Folding

COMPENDIUM
PART 3

IRIS
Folding
COMPENDIUM
PART 3

**Maruscha Gaasenbeek
and Tine Beauveser**

FORTE PUBLISHERS

© 2006 Forte Uitgevers, Utrecht
© 2006 for the translation by the publisher

ISBN 90 5877 648 4

This is a publication from
Forte Publishers BV
P.O. Box 1394
3500 BJ Utrecht
The Netherlands

For more information about the creative books
available from Forte Uitgevers:
www.forteuitgevers.nl

Photography and digital image editing:
Fotografie Gerhard Witteveen,
Apeldoorn, the Netherlands
Cover and inner design:
BADE creatieve communicatie, Baarn,
the Netherlands
Translation:
Michael Ford, TextCase,
Hilversum, the Netherlands

Contents

Preface

Colourful paper and a simple folding technique form the irresistible combination which everybody knows as Iris folding. This compendium contains the books *Iris Folding for Celebrations* and *Colourful Folding* written by Maruscha Gaasenbeek and Tine Beauveser, and the book *Iris Folding Stylish Greeting Cards* written by Maruscha Gaasenbeek.

The cards in this book are filled with strips cut from the inside of normal envelopes, Iris folding paper, origami paper, holographic paper and English and Italian luxury paper. The more choice of paper you have, the more attractive the cards become. You use the colourful strips of paper to cover the opening in the card by following the numbered sections of the pattern. You will create a new piece of art every time. Sometimes the card will have bright contrasts in colour and other times the colours will be in soft tints.

You will surprise your family and friends with your attractive creations and you will have lots of fun making spectacular Iris folding cards.

Good luck,

Maruscha   Tine

Techniques

The starting point for Iris folding is the pattern. Cut the outline of the pattern out of the back of your card and then fill the hole from the outside to the inside with folded strips of paper. You work at the back of the card, so you work, in fact, on a mirror image. When you have finished the Iris folding, stick the card onto another card. For a glass or a diamond shape, select four different sheets of paper for an hexagonal shape select six different sheets of paper whose patterns and colours combine and contrast each other nicely. Cut all the paper into strips in the same way, for example, from left to right. Depending on the pattern, you will need between four and eight strips. The width of the strips also depends on the pattern and is stated for each card. You need to first fold the edge of the strips over and then sort them into the different colours. Next, cover each section in turn by following the numbers (1, 2, 3, 4, 5, etc.) using a different colour each time. Lay the strips down with the fold facing towards the middle of the pattern and stick the left and right-hand sides to the card using adhesive tape. Finally, use an attractive piece of holographic paper to cover the hole in the middle.

The hexagon, the diamond and the basic shape

It is important to start with the basic hexagon, the basic diamond and the basic shape, because from this, you will learn the unique folding and sticking technique needed for all the patterns. You will notice that you quickly get used to the technique of Iris folding.

Preparation
The hexagon (page 14 Step-by-step)

1. Lay a piece of ice blue card (13 x 9.7 cm) down with the back facing towards you.
2. With the aid of a light box, draw the outline of the hexagon onto the card using a pencil an cut it out.
3. Stick a copy of the hexagon shown in this book (pattern 1) to your cutting mat using adhesive tape.
4. Place the card with the hole on the pattern (you should be looking at the back of the card) and only stick the left-hand side of the card to your cutting mat using masking tape.
5. Select six different sheets of paper. Two blue envelopes and four sheets of Iris Folding paper have been used for the card on page 14.
6. Cut 2 cm wide strips from these sheets and make separate piles of colour A, colour B, colour C, colour D, colour E and colour F.
7. Fold the edge of each strip over (approximately 0.7 cm wide) with the nice side facing outwards.

The diamond (page 14 Step-by-step)

1. Lay the violet card (13.5 x 8 cm) down with the back facing towards you.
2. With the aid of a light box, copy the diamond onto the card using a pencil and cut it out.
3. Stick a copy of the diamond shown in this book

(pattern 1) to your cutting mat using adhesive tape.

4. Place the card with the hole on the pattern (you should be looking at the back of the card) and only stick the left-hand side of the card to your cutting mat using masking tape.
5. Select four different sheets of paper. One red envelope, one blue envelope, origami paper with blue lilies and paper with red castles have been used for the card in the bottom right-hand corner of page 14.
6. Cut 2 cm wide strips from these pieces of paper and make separate piles of colour A, colour B, colour C and colour D.
7. Fold the edge of each strip over (approximately 0.7 cm wide) with the nice side facing outwards.

The basic shape (page 15 Step-by-Step)
1. Lay a piece of white card (13.8 x 10 cm) down with the back facing towards you.
2. With the aid of a light box, copy the basic -shape onto the card using a pencil and cut it out.
3. Stick a copy of the basic pattern given in this book (pattern 1) to your cutting mat using adhesive tape.
4. Place the card with the hole on the pattern (you should be looking at the back of the card) and only stick the left-hand side of the card to your cutting mat using masking tape.
5. Choose four sheets of beige and brown paper, each with different patterns. Two envelopes and two sheets of IRIS folding paper have been used

for the card in the bottom right-hand corner of page 15.
6. Cut 2 cm wide strips from these pieces of paper and make separate piles of colour A, colour B, colour C and colour D.
7. Fold the edge of each strip over (approximately 0.7 cm wide) with the nice side facing outwards.

Iris Folding
The hexagon
1. Take a folded strip of colour A and place it over section one, exactly against the line of the pattern with the folded edge facing towards the middle. Allow 0.5 cm to stick out on the left and right-hand sides and cut the rest off. By doing so, the strip will also slightly stick out over the edge of the pattern at the bottom, so that section 1 is totally covered.
2. Stick the strip to the card on the left and right-hand sides using a small piece of adhesive tape, but remain 0.5 cm from the edge of the card.
3. Take a strip of colour B and place it on section 2 of the pattern. Tape the left and right-hand sides to the card.
4. Take a strip of colour C. Place it on section 3 and stick it into place.
5. Take a strip of colour D. Place it on section 4 and stick it into place.
6. Take a strip of colour E. Place this on section 5 and stick it into place. Finally, take a strip of colour F and stick it onto section 6.

7. Continue with colour A on section 7, colour B on section 8, colour C on section 9, colour D on section 10, colour E on section 11 and colour F on section 12.

The strips on sections 1, 7, 13, 19, 25, 31 and 37 of this pattern are all of colour A. The strips on sections 2, 8, 14, 20, 26, 32 and 38 are all of colour B. The strips on sections 3, 9, 15, 21, 27, 33 and 39 are all of colour C. The strips on sections 4, 10, 16, 22, 28, 34 and 40 are all of colour D. The strips on sections 5, 11, 17, 23, 29, 35 and 41 are all of colour E. The strips on sections 6, 12, 18, 24, 30, 36 and 42 are all of colour F.

Finishing

Carefully remove the card after finishing section 42. Stick a piece of holographic paper in the middle on the back of the card. You can use punches, figure scissors and bits of paper to add extra finishing touches to the card. Stick small pieces of double-sided adhesive tape along the edges or use foam tape to bridge the height difference. Remove the protective layer from the double-sided adhesive tape and stick your design on a double card. Do not use glue, because all the paper strips place pressure on the card.

The diamond

1. Take a folded strip of colour A and place it upside down over section 1, exactly against the line of the pattern with the folded edge facing towards the middle. Allow 0.5 cm to stick out on the left and right-hand sides and cut the rest off. By doing so, the strip will also slightly stick out over the edge of the pattern at the bottom, so that section 1 is totally covered.

2. Stick the strip to the card on the left and right-hand sides using a small piece of adhesive tape, but remain 0.5 cm from the edge of the card.

3. Take a strip of colour B and place it on section 2 of the pattern. Tape the left and right-hand sides to the card.

4. Take a strip of colour C. Place this on section 3 and stick it into place.

5. Take a strip of colour D. Place this on section 4 and stick it into place.

6. Start again with colour A on section 5, colour B on section 6, colour C on section 7 and colour D on section 8.

The strips on sections 1, 5, 9 and 13 of this pattern are all of colour A. The strips on sections 2, 6, 10 and 14 are all of colour B. The strips on sections 3, 7, 11 and 15 are all of colour C. The strips on sections 4, 8, 12 and 16 are all of colour D.

Finishing

Carefully remove the card after finishing section 16. Stick a piece of holographic paper in the middle on the back of the card. You can use punches, figure scissors and bits of paper to add extra finishing touches to the card. Stick small pieces of double-sided adhesive tape along the edges or use foam tape to bridge the height difference. Remove the protective layer from the double-sided adhesive tape and stick your design on a double card. Do not use glue, because all the paper strips place pressure on the card.

The basic shape

1. Take a folded strip of colour A and place it over section 1, exactly against the line of the pattern with the folded edge facing towards the middle. Allow 0.5 cm to stick out on the left and right-hand sides and cut off the rest. By doing so, the strip will also slightly stick out over the edge of the pattern at the bottom, so that section 1 is totally covered.
2. Stick the strip to the card on the left and right-hand sides using a small piece of adhesive tape, but remain 0.5 cm from the edge of the card.
3. Take a strip of colour B and place it on -section 2 of the pattern. Tape the left and right-hand sides to the card.
4. Take a strip of colour C. Place this on section 3 and stick it into place.
5. Take a strip of colour D. Place this on section 4 and stick it into place.
6. Start again with colour A on section 5, colour B on section 6, colour C on section 7 and colour D on section 8.

The strips on sections 1, 5, 9, 13 and 17 of this pattern are all of colour A. The strips on sections 2, 6, 10, 14 and 18 are all of colour B. The strips on sections 3, 7, 11, 15 and 19 are all of colour C. The strips on sections 4, 8, 12, 16 and 20 are all of colour D.

Finishing

Carefully remove the card after finishing section 20. Stick a piece of holographic paper in the middle on the back of the card. You can use punches, corner scissors and bits of paper to add extra finishing touches to the card. Stick small pieces of double-sided adhesive tape along the edges. Remove the protective layer and stick your design on a double card. Do not use glue, because all the paper strips place pressure on the card.

Embossing

To emboss, place the stencil on the good side of the card and stick it in place using masking tape. Place the card (with the stencil) upside-down on a light box and carefully push the paper through the stencil's opening using the embossing stylus. You only have to push along the edges to raise the entire image.

Rub the point of the embossing stylus with a candle so that it glides smoothly over the paper.

Punch cards

When using punch cards, the order in which you make the card may differ to that given in the book. For cards where you cut out the pattern yourself, the separate, cut-out parts are stuck on at the end, whilst the parts are covered first for punch cards. For that you need a big piece of paper that you do not fold and that you cut to size only on the same side as the strip.

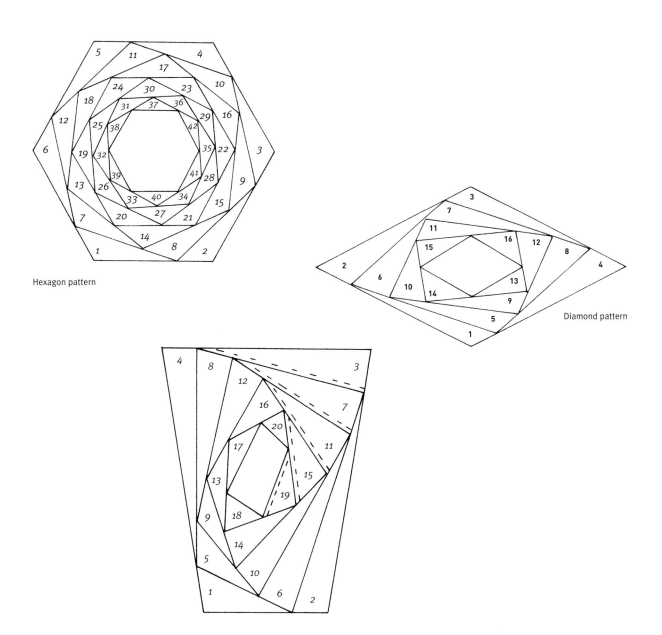

Hexagon pattern

Diamond pattern

Basic shape pattern

Materials

To make the cards:

- ❏ Card: Canson Mi-Teintes (C), Artoz (A), Papicolor (P), cArt-us (cA) and Romak (R)
- ❏ Separating sheets from K&Company
- ❏ Pergamano Parchment separating sheets
- ❏ Iris folding text stickers
- ❏ Iris folding greetings sheets
- ❏ Borders & Corners paper (Sharon Ann)
- ❏ Knife and cutting mat
- ❏ Ruler with a metal cutting edge (Securit)
- ❏ Adhesive tape
- ❏ Double-sided adhesive tape and foam tape
- ❏ Masking tape
- ❏ Various punches (TomTas, MakeMe!, Media, Carl, Lim)
- ❏ Various corner punches (MakeMe!, Fiskars, Carl, Lim, Reuser)
- ❏ Border ornament punches (Fiskars, Vaessen)
- ❏ 2-in-1 border punch (Media)
- ❏ 3-in-1 corner punch (Fiskars)
- ❏ Punch with exchangeable shapes (TomTas)
- ❏ Scissors and silhouette scissors
- ❏ Corner scissors (Fiskars)
- ❏ Figure scissors (Fiskars, Reuser)
- ❏ Embossing stencils (Marianne Design)
- ❏ Embossing light box
- ❏ Embossing stylus
- ❏ Hole punch
- ❏ Candle
- ❏ Ornare pricking template (Marianne Design)
- ❏ Pricking mat and pricking pen
- ❏ Vellum
- ❏ Ridge Master
- ❏ Photo glue
- ❏ Black fine-liner
- ❏ Pencil

Iris folding

- ❏ Strips of used envelopes
- ❏ Strips of Iris folding paper
- ❏ Strips of de luxe Iris folding paper
- ❏ Strips of holographic paper (Em-Je)
- ❏ English and Italian paper from Damen (D) and Vlieger (V) (50 x 70 cm or 70 x 100 cm)
- ❏ Japanese paper
- ❏ Origami paper from Ori-Expres (O-E)
- ❏ Gift paper

The middle of the card

- ❏ Holographic paper

The patterns

Full-size examples of all the patterns are give in this book. Use a light box to draw round the outside. The shapes are usually easy to cut out of card. Specially punched cards are available for the wine glass, the pinecone, the Celtic star, the holly leaf and the hourglass, the duck, the sweetjar, the dragonfly, the cross pattern and the Christmas decoration, the cat, the dog, the small feeding bottle, the jug and the four-leaf clover.

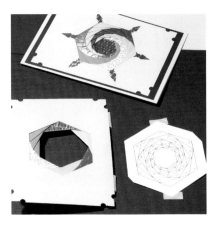

Hexagon

1. Cut the hexagon out of the back of a piece of card. Cut the Iris folding paper and the envelopes into strips and fold the edge over.

2. Stick the pattern to your cutting mat. Place the card on top and tape the left-hand side to the cutting mat. Place the fold of the strips exactly against the line and stick down the left and right-hand sides using adhesive tape.

3. Fold the card open from time to time to see whether the patterns continue nicely.

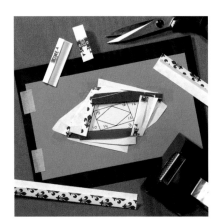

Diamond

1. Cut the diamond out of the back of a piece of card.

2. Cut the chosen paper into strips and fold a border along the entire length of each strip. Stick the pattern to your cutting mat. Place the card on top and tape the left-hand side to the cutting mat.

3. Place the fold of the strips exactly against the line and stick down the left and right-hand sides using adhesive tape. Fold the card open from time to time to see whether the patterns continue nicely.

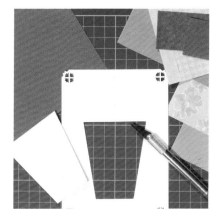

Basic shape

1. Iris folding paper and envelopes: the perfect combination.

2. Cut the basic shape out of the back of the card. Cut the Iris folding paper into strips and fold the edge over.

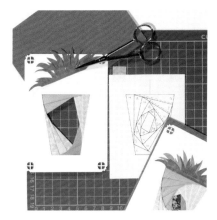

3. Stick the pattern to your cutting mat. Place the card on top and tape the left-hand side to the cutting mat. Place the fold of the strips exactly against the line and stick down the left and right-hand sides using adhesive tape.

4. Fold the card open from time to time to see whether the pattern you have made continues nicely.

Cards based on the hexagon

Gefeliciteerd

Hexagons

Ice-cold sparkle

on winter cards.

All the cards are made according to the instructions given for the basic pattern (see Techniques).

Card 1 - Basic pattern

Card: pink A481 (14.8 x 21 cm), dark blue A417 (14 x 10 cm) and ice blue P42 (13 x 9.7 cm) • Pattern 1 • 2 cm wide strips from 2 blue envelopes and from 4 sheets of Iris folding paper (blue, red and de luxe pastels sets) • Silver holographic paper (Em-Je) • Spindle figure scissors • Arrow corner punch
Punch the corners of the smallest card and cut out the hexagon. After completing the Iris folding, cut the points for the ice-crystal. To do so, make an incision in the holographic paper with the figure scissors, turn the scissors over and then, approximately 0.5 cm away from the incision, cut upwards at an angle to produce a point.

Card 2

Card: pastel green A331 (14.8 x 21 cm), dark blue A417 (14 x 9.5 cm) and white (13.6 x 9.1 cm) • Pattern 1 • 6 groups of 2 cm wide strips from 4 sheets of Iris folding paper (blue, purple, petrol and de luxe pastels sets) • Silver holographic paper • Vulcano figure scissors • Snowflakes 3-in-1 corner punch
For the points, fold a strip of holographic paper double, cut it at an angle once with the figure scissors and once with normal scissors. Fold it open and stick it on the card.

Card 3

Card: white (14.8 x 21 cm) and light blue C490 (14.8 x 9.2 cm) • Pattern 1 • 6 groups of 2 cm wide strips from 3 blue envelopes and from 2 Iris folding sheets (blue and petrol sets) • Silver holographic paper • Bells border picture punch

Card 4

Card: indigo C140 (14.8 x 21 cm) and white (13.8 x 10 cm) • Pattern 1 • 2 cm wide strips from 5 blue envelopes and from 1 sheet of Iris folding paper (blue set) • Silver holographic paper • Heartstrings figure scissors • Star-border ornament punch

Card 5

Card: azure A393 (13 x 26 cm), night blue P41 (12 x 12 cm) and Stars silver holographic paper (12.3 x 12.3 cm) • Pattern 1 • 6 groups of 2 cm wide strips from 1 blue envelope and from 5 sheets of Iris folding paper (aqua set) • Silver holographic paper • Seagull figure scissors • Snowflakes 3-in-1 corner punch

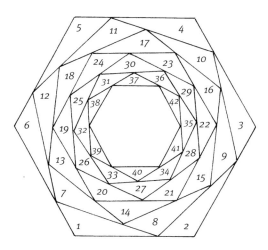

Pattern 1 - Basic shape

sets and a Christmas Iris folding greetings sheet)
• *Superstencil MD SU 4002* • *Silver thread* • *Silver holographic paper*
Prick the embroidery cardboard. Emboss the edges and cut the hexagon out of the white card. Embroider the diamond pattern and fill the ice-crystal with strips.

Card 6

Card: white (13 x 26 cm and 10 x 10 cm) • Dotted parchment 1643 (12 x 12 cm) and lavender blue 1602 (11 x 11 cm) • Pattern 1 • 6 groups of 2 cm wide strips from 4 envelopes (pink, blue and grey)
• Silver Holographic paper • Heartbeat figure scissors

Card 7

Card: azure P04 (14.8 x 21 cm) and metallic white (13.8 x 9.7 cm) • Pattern 1 • 2 cm wide strips from 2 envelopes (grey and blue) and from 3 sheets of Iris folding paper (de luxe colourful and pastels

Playing with hexagons

Cheers!

The cognac glass is made according to the instructions given for card 1. Note: whilst Iris folding, the hexagon will change into a square.

Card 1

Card: mango P40 (13 x 26 cm), metallic golden brown P144 (11.5 x 11.5 cm), brick red P35 (11.1 x 11.1 cm) and light beige C340 (10.5 x 10.5 cm) • Pattern 2 • 6 groups of 2 cm wide strips from 5 sheets of Iris folding paper (orange, yellow and de luxe pastels sets) • Bronze holographic paper

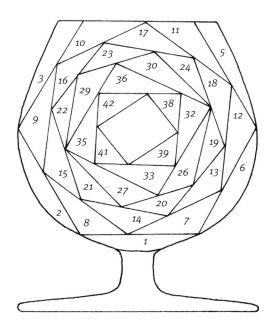

Pattern 2 - Cognac glass

Cut the goblet, without the stem and the foot, out of the smallest card. Use a light box to copy the stem and the foot onto a strip of brown Iris folding paper. Cut it out and stick it below the goblet. To avoid making a mistake, read these instructions first and use 6 coloured pencils to mark the sections of your copy of the pattern with the correct colours. Colour D (pink) is not included in the first round of Iris folding.

Colour A (dark brown) will be in sections 1, 7, 13 and 19 and will then stop. There are no sections 25, 31 and 37. Colour D (pink) will be in sections 10, 16, and 22 and will then stop. There are no sections 4, 28, 34 and 40.

Once a colour is no longer going to be used, remove the strips from the table and continue with the other colours.

Card 2

Card: dark brown P38 (13 x 26 cm), metallic golden brown P144 (12 x 12 cm) and white (11 x 11 cm) • Pattern 2 • 2 cm wide strips from 2 brown envelopes and from 4 sheets of Iris folding paper (yellow, red and de luxe Christmas sets) • Bronze holographic paper • Regal corner scissors

Card 3

Card: dark brown (13 x 26 cm), gold P102 (11.6 x 11.6 cm) and white C335 (10.7 x 10.7 cm) • Pattern 2 • 2 cm wide strips from 1 cloudy envelope and from 5 sheets of Iris folding paper (yellow, orange and red sets) • Gold holographic paper • Leaves 3-in-1 corner punch
Punch the top corners of the white card and cut out the goblet.

Card 4

Card: salmon beige C384 (13 x 26 cm) and rust (12 x 12 cm) • Pattern 2 • 2 cm wide strips from 6 beige/ brown envelopes • Gold holographic paper • Reuser multi corner punch
Punch the top corners of the rust card and cut out the goblet.

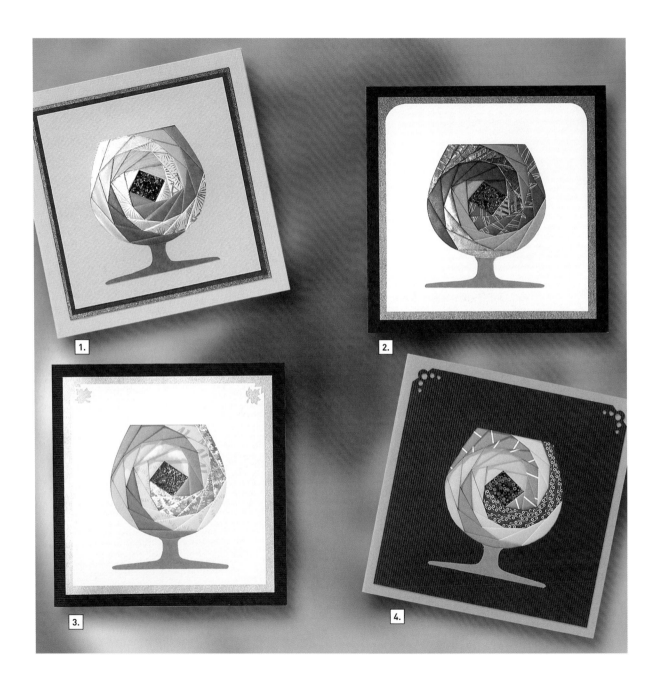

Guitar and musical note

Music gives colour to your life.

The guitar is made according to the description given for card 1 and the musical note is made according to the description given for card 5.

Card 1

Card: caramel P26 (14.8 x 21 cm), metallic golden brown P144 (14 x 9.6 cm) and white (14 x 6.7 cm) • Pattern 3 • 2 cm wide strips from 4 sheets of Iris folding paper (orange and yellow sets) • Gold holographic paper • Musical notes border punch

Cut the guitar, without the stem, out of the white card. Note: colour A (bronze) stops after section 21b. There are no sections 25 and 29.

For colour B (brown), there is no section 22, nor section 30, but there is a section 26. Copy half of the ring and half of the stem onto a strip of colour B. Fold them double and cut them out.

Stick the ring in the middle and stick the stem over the ring. Punch the edges of the brown card.

Card 2

Card: petrol (14.8 x 21 cm) and white (14.3 x 9 cm) • Pattern 3 • 4 groups of 2 cm wide strips from 2 green envelopes and from 2 sheets of Iris folding paper (petrol set) • Silver holographic paper • Music multi corner punch

Card 3

Card: pale yellow P29 (14.8 x 21 cm) and nut brown P39 (14.8 x 8 cm) • Pattern 3 • 2 cm wide strips from 2 brown envelopes and from 2 sheets of Iris folding paper (orange and de luxe pastels sets) • Gold holographic paper • Decorations from a Music multi corner punch

Card 4

Card: brick red C130 (14.8 x 21 cm) and white (13.7 x 10 cm) • Sheet of burgundy Iris folding paper from the red set (14.2 x 10 cm) • Pattern 3 • 2 cm wide strips from 4 sheets of Iris folding paper (Avec set) • Silver holographic paper

Cut a strip of 6 x 3.5 cm and a strip of 7 x 4 cm off of the white card.

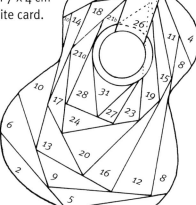

Pattern 3 - Guitar

Card 5

*Card: gold line P301 (14.8 x 21 cm) and brick red
C130 (13.3 x 9.1 cm) • Pattern 4 • 2 cm wide strips
from 1 brown envelope, from 1 sheet of music paper
and from 2 sheets of Iris folding paper (purple and
de luxe pastels sets) • De luxe Iris folding paper
(7 x 3.5 cm) for the stem • Music paper (13.3 x 1 cm)
• Bronze holographic paper*
Cut out the circle from the note and fill it with
strips.

Card 6

*Card: Structura cherry red P133 (14.8 x 21 cm) and
metallic white (13 x 8.8 cm) • Stars holographic
paper (13.5 x 9.3 cm) • Pattern 4 • 2 cm wide strips
from 2 red envelopes and from 2 grey envelopes
• Red paper (7 x 3.5 cm) for the stem • Stars
holographic paper*

Card 7

*Card: dark green A309 (14.8 x 21 cm) and pastel
green A331 (13.3 x 9 cm) • Pattern 4 • 2 cm wide
strips from 2 envelopes (purple and green) and
from 2 sheets of Iris folding paper (petrol and de
luxe pastels sets) • Purple paper (7 x 3.5 cm) for
the stem • Silver holographic paper • Music
border punch*

Card 8

*Card: grey C431 (14.8 x 21 cm), bright red C506
(14 x 10 cm) and white (13.7 x 9.5 cm) • Pattern 4*

*• 2 cm wide strips from 4 grey and dark blue
envelopes • Grey paper (7 x 3.5 cm) for the stem*
• Silver holographic paper • Accolade corner punch
• Musical note figure punch

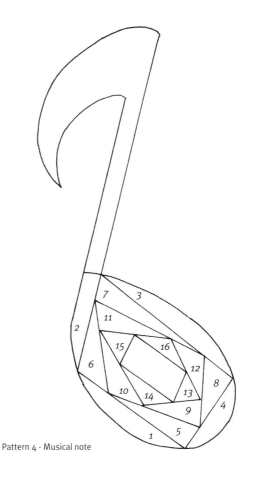

Pattern 4 - Musical note

Flags and sweets

Let's celebrate!

The flags are made according to the description given for card 1 and the sweets are made according to the description given for card 5.

Card 1

Card: pastel blue A413 (14.8 x 21 cm), corn-flower A425 (13.8 x 9.5 cm) and sky blue A391 (13.3 x 9 cm) • Pattern 5 • 1.5 cm wide strips from 3 sheets of Iris folding paper (blue and purple sets) • Silver holographic paper • Flowers 3-in-1 corner punch • Hole punch for the top of the flag pole
Cut the flags, without the poles, out of the smallest card.

Card 2

Card: white (14.8 x 21 cm and 9.7 x 7.5 cm) and fiesta red P12 (13 x 9.7 cm) • Hearts vellum (Heyda) (11.5 x 9.1 cm) • Pattern 5 • 1.5 cm wide strips from 3 sheets of Iris folding paper (green and de luxe flowers sets) • Silver holographic paper • Girl figure punch • Hole punch

Card 3

Card: Structura pale yellow P132 (14.8 x 21 cm), Iris blue P31 (14 x 9.8 cm) and spring green P08 (13.6 x 8.6 cm) • 2 strips (13.6 x 1 cm) from a blue Iris folding greetings sheet • Pattern 5 • 1.5 cm

wide strips from 2 envelopes (blue and green) and from 1 sheet of Iris folding paper (blue set) • Silver holographic paper • Hearts from a heart border ornament punch • Hole punch

Card 4

Card: white (14.8 x 21 cm) and fiesta red P12 (10.8 x 8.4 cm) • Sweet -vellum (Heyda) (14.8 x 21 cm) • Pattern 5 • 3 groups of 1.5 cm wide strips from 2 red envelopes and from a red Iris folding greetings sheet • Number 4 from Juliana Die-Cut Alphabet • Silver holographic paper • Hole punch

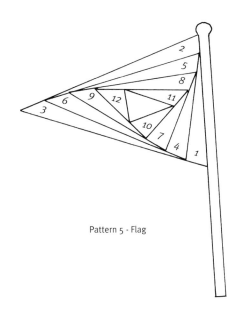

Pattern 5 - Flag

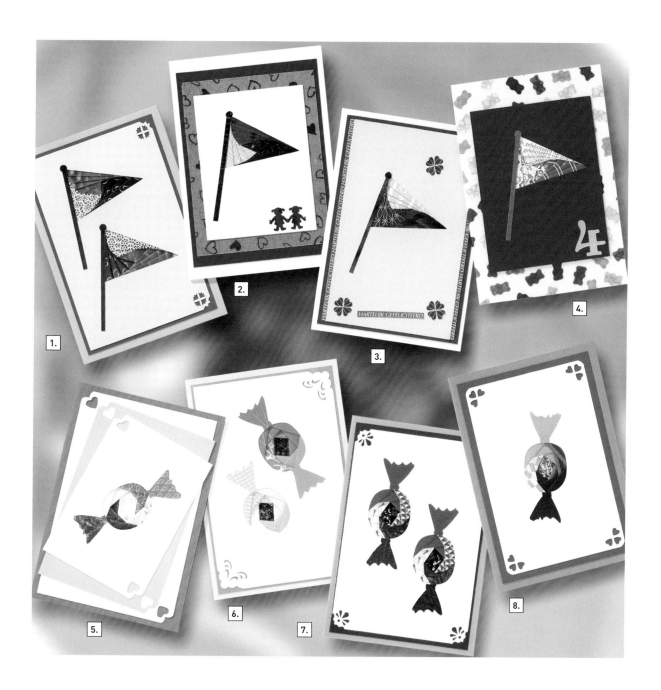

Card 5

Card: pine green A339 (14.8 x 21 cm), Structura fern green P137 (12.5 x 8.3 cm) and white (14 x 9.5 cm and 10.7 x 7.5 cm) • Pattern 6 • 1.5 cm wide strips from 4 sheets of Iris folding paper (green and yellow sets) • 2 pieces of green Iris folding paper (3 x 3 cm) for the bows • Green holographic paper • Multi corner punch

Punch two corners of each single card and cut the sweet, without the bows, out of the smallest card. Use a light box to copy the bows.

Card 6

Card: Structura sunflower P134 (14.8 x 21 cm) and white (13.8 x 9.5 cm) • Orange Iris folding paper (14.2 x 9.8 cm) • Pattern 6 • 1.5 cm wide strips from 4 yellow and 4 orange envelopes • 4 pieces of envelope paper (3 x 3 cm) • Gold holographic paper • Fountain corner punch

Card 7

Card: mango A575 (14.8 x 21 cm), bright orange (14.2 x 9.8 cm) and white (13.5 x 9.5 cm) • Pattern 6 • 4 groups of 1.5 cm wide strips from 2 red envelopes and from 2 sheets of Iris folding paper (red set) • 4 pieces of red paper • Rainbow holographic paper • Multi corner punch

Card 8

Card: violet P20 (14.8 x 21 cm), cornflower A425 (13.8 x 9.5 cm) and white (12.8 x 8.5 cm) • Pattern 6 • 1.5 cm wide strips from 4 purple envelopes • 2 pieces of paper (3 x 3 cm) • Silver holographic paper • Hearts 3-in-1 corner punch

Pattern 6 - Sweet

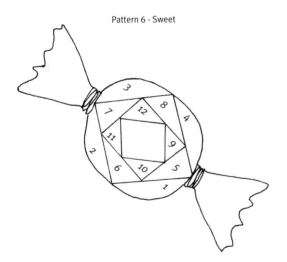

Celtic star

A chic star.

All the cards are made according to the instructions given for card 1.

Card 2
Card: dark blue A417 (13 x 26 cm) and white (11.3 x 11.3 cm) • Pattern 7 • 2 cm wide strips from 1 green envelope and from 3 sheets of Iris folding paper (petrol and de luxe colourful sets) • Silver holographic paper • Lily corner punch (Carl)
Punch the corners of the white card.

Card 1 (card on the cover)
Card: azure P04 (13 x 26 cm), white (12 x 12 cm) and dark blue P06 (11.7 x 11.7 cm) • Pattern 7 • 2 cm wide strips from 3 envelopes (yellow, grey and blue) and from 1 sheet of Iris folding paper (aqua set) • Silver holographic paper • Celestial 3-in-1 corner punch
Punch the corners of the smallest card and cut out the four points of the star. First, cover the striped sections around the middle with the yellow strips and then use the other three colours for the Iris folding. Cut a yellow circle (Ø 1.7 cm) and stick it on the front of the card.

Card 3

Card: white (13 x 26 cm and 11 x 11 cm) and purple P46 (11.9 x 11.9 cm) • Pattern 7 • 2 cm wide strips from 4 sheets of Iris folding paper (red and purple sets) • Gold holographic paper • Iris folding text sticker
When you have finished the Iris folding, stick a red circle in the middle.

Card 4

Card: Structura pale yellow P132 (13 x 26 cm), honey yellow A243 (11.8 x 11.8 cm) and night blue P41 (11.8 x 11.8 cm) • Pattern 7 • 2 cm wide strips from 3 yellow envelopes and from 1 sheet of Iris folding paper (de luxe Christmas set) • Gold stars holographic paper • Star corner punch
Use the gold paper to cover the striped sections in the middle. Also use it to make the circle in the middle.

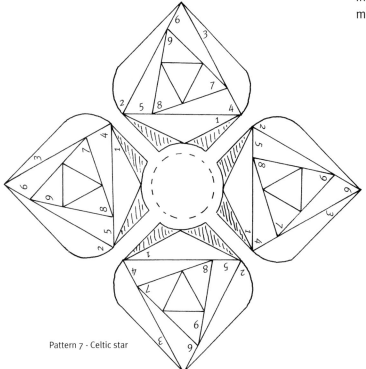

Pattern 7 - Celtic star

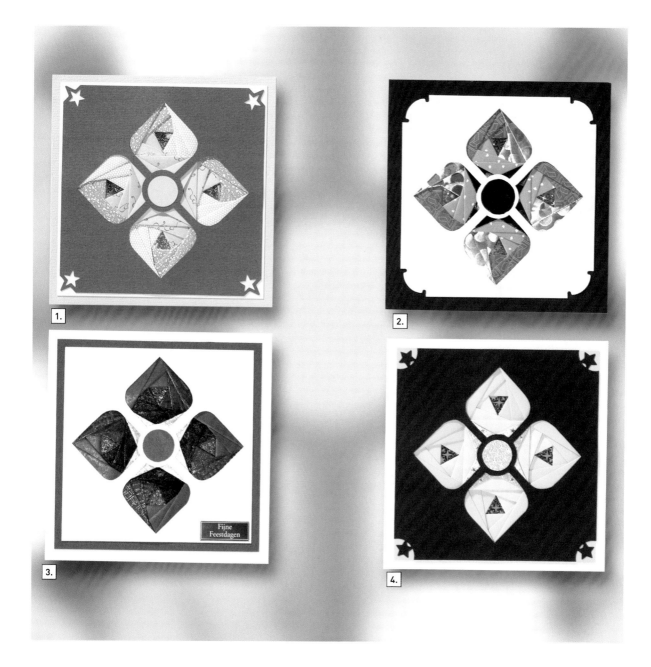

1.

2.

3.

Fijne
Feestdagen

4.

Pinecone and holly

Autumn and Christmas.

The pinecones are made according to the description given for card 1 and the holly leaves are made according to the description given for card 2.

Card 1 (card on the cover)

Card: dark green A309 (14.8 x 21 cm) and white (13.8 x 9.5 cm) • Pattern 8 • 2 cm wide strips from 4 sheets of Iris folding paper (petrol and aqua sets) • Silver holographic paper • Accolade corner punch

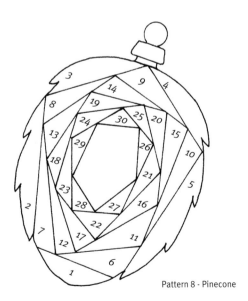

Pattern 8 · Pinecone

Punch the corners of the white card. Cut out the pinecone without the suspension eye. After finishing the Iris folding, cut the suspension eye out of holographic paper and stick it on the card.

Card 2

Card: mint green (14.8 x 21 cm), metallic emerald P143 (13.2 x 9.5 cm) and white (12 x 8.5 cm) • Pattern 9 • 5 groups of 2 cm wide strips from 2 green envelopes and from 2 sheets of Iris folding paper (petrol and green sets) • Silver holographic paper • Berries from a hole punch • Holly corner punch

Punch the corners of the white card and cut out the leaf without the stem. After finishing the Iris folding, cut out the stem and stick it on the card together with the berries.

Card 3

Card: dark green A309 (13 x 26 cm), pastel green A331 (10.6 x 10.6 cm), dark blue A417 (10 x 10 cm), metallic emerald P143 (9.1 x 9.1 cm) and white (8.5 x 8.5 cm) • Pattern 8 • 5 groups of 2 cm wide strips from 1 turquoise envelope and from 3 sheets of Iris folding paper (petrol and de luxe pastels sets) • Silver holographic paper

Card 4

Card: Christmas green P18 (14.8 x 21 cm), silvery grey (13.8 x 9.3 cm) and white (13 x 8.5 cm) • Pattern 9 • 5 groups of 2 cm wide strips from

4 sheets of Iris folding paper (blue and petrol sets) • Piece of Iris folding paper (5 x 8 cm - petrol set) for the second leaf • Silver holo-graphic paper

Card 5

Card: cerise P33 (14.8 x 21 cm), burgundy (13.8 x 10 cm) and metallic white (12.8 x 9 cm) • Pattern 8 • 2 cm wide strips from 2 sheets of holographic paper (stars and holly) and from 3 sheets of Iris folding paper (red and purple sets) • Silver holographic paper • Bow border picture punch

Card 6

Card: white (14.8 x 21 cm and 11 x 6.7 cm), Perla gold P141 (12.9 x 8.7 cm) and red (12.3 x 8 cm) • Pattern 9 • 5 groups of 2 cm wide strips from 4 sheets of Iris folding paper (petrol and green sets) • Hole punch • Gold holographic paper

Card 7

Card: ivory C111 (13 x 26 cm and 8 x 8 cm) and brick red P35 (11 x 11 cm) • Piece of Iris folding paper (11.4 x 11.4 cm - green set) • Pattern 9 • 5 groups of 2 cm wide strips from 1 red envelope, from 1 beige envelope and from 2 sheets of Iris folding paper (green set) • Hole punch • Gold holographic paper

Card 8

Card: brick red P35 (14.8 x 21 cm) and ivory C111 (13.7 x 9.5 cm) • Pattern 8 • 2 cm wide strips from 1 orange envelope and from 4 sheets of Iris folding paper (yellow and orange sets) • 2 strips of 9.5 cm Borders & Corners Oak Leaf/Plaid paper • Gold holographic paper

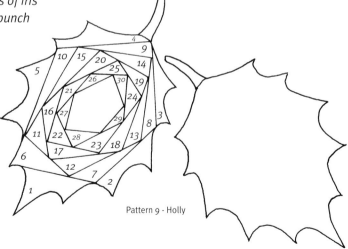

Pattern 9 - Holly

Pumpkins

Why don't you make a Halloween card?

All the cards are made according to the instructions given for card 1.

Card 1

Card: mango A575 (13 x 26 cm), Iris blue P31 (12.6 x 12.6 cm) and metallic golden brown P144 (11 x 11 cm) • Dotted parchment 1643 (12.2 x 12.2 cm) • Pattern 10 • 2.5 cm wide strips from 6 sheets of Iris folding paper (orange, purple and green sets) • 2 pieces of paper (7 x 4 cm) for the sides and 1 piece of gold paper (3 x 4 cm) for the stem • Witch figure punch • Celestial 3-in-1 corner punch

Cut the pumpkin, without the stem and the sides, out of the smallest card. Read these instructions first and then colour the sections on the copy of the pumpkin pattern using coloured pencils. Note: colour A (purple) is not used after section 25 and there are no sections 31 and 37. Colour C (pink) is not used after section 27 and there are no sections 33 and 39. Colour E (brown) is not used after section 29 and there are no sections 35 and 41. After section 30, you only continue with colours B, D and F. Cut the top edge of strip 34b using the figure scissors and stick eyes on strips 38 and 42.

After finishing the Iris folding, use a light box to copy the sides and the stem. Cut them out and stick them on the front of the card.

Card 2

Card: pastel green A331 (13 x 26 cm), lemon P09 (12.2 x 12.2 cm) and sea green (12 x 12 cm) • Pattern 10 • 2.5 cm wide strips from 1 green envelope and from 5 sheets of Iris folding paper (yellow and green sets) • Green paper (two pieces 7 x 4 cm and one piece 3 x 4 cm) • Gold holographic paper • Iris folding text sticker • Star figure punches • Arrow corner punch

Card 3

Card: wine red P36 (13 x 26 cm) and Structura orange P135 (11 x 11 cm) • Iris folding paper (11.3 x 11.3 cm - de luxe flowers set) • Pattern 10 • 6 groups of 2.5 cm wide strips from 4 sheets of Iris folding paper (red, yellow and de luxe flowers sets) • Red Iris folding paper (7 x 8 cm) • Rainbow holographic paper • Accolade corner punch • Star punch

Card 4

Card: fawn A241 (13 x 26 cm), grey blue C354 (12.2 x 12.2 cm) and wine red P36 (11.5 x 12 cm) • Pattern 10 • 6 groups of 2.5 cm strips from 5 envelopes (ochre, beige, grey and burgundy) and from 1 sheet of Iris folding paper (green set) • Ochre paper (7 x 8 cm) • 2 strips of Borders & Corners Pine/Gingham paper (12 x 0.6 cm) • Gold holographic paper • Mini shell figure scissors

Card 5

Card: lobster red A545 (13 x 26 cm), gold P300 (12 x 12 cm), crimson A549 (11.5 x 11.5 cm) and white (11 x 11 cm) • Pattern 10 • 6 groups of 2.5 cm wide strips from 1 yellow envelope and from 4 sheets of Iris folding paper (orange and yellow sets) • Orange paper (7 x 8 cm) • Gold holographic paper • Borders and Corners Red Oak paper

Card 6

Card: black A219 (13 x 26 cm) and olive green P45 (11 x 11 cm) • Lime green Fantasy parchment 1600 (12.5 x 12.5 cm) and light green paper (11.6 x 11.6 cm) • Pattern 10 • 2.5 cm wide strips from 6 sheets of Iris folding paper (green set) • Green paper (7 x 8 cm) • Green holographic paper • Celestial 3-in-1 corner punch

Card 7

Card: gold line P301 (13 x 26 cm) and cognac brown (10 x 10 cm) • Pale yellow parchment 1645 (12 x 12 cm) • Pattern 10 • 6 groups of 2.5 cm wide strips from 5 sheets of Iris folding paper (yellow and green sets) • Gold paper (7 x 8 cm) • Gold holographic paper • Heartbeat figure scissors • Witch figure punch

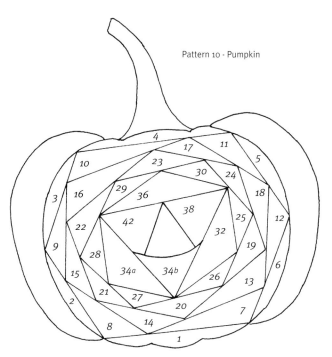

Pattern 10 - Pumpkin

Hourglass and wine glass

Best wishes!

The hourglass is made according to the description given for card 1. The wine glass is made according to the description given for card 4.

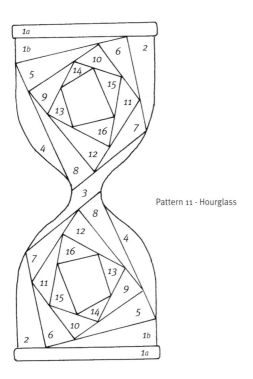

Pattern 11 - Hourglass

Card 1

Card: white (14.8 x 21 cm) and wine red (14.2 x 10 cm - 120 gram) • Pattern 11 • 2 cm wide strips from 4 beige/white envelopes • Gold holographic paper • Asiatic symbol punch

Turn the punch upside down and punch all the corners of the red paper twice with part of the pattern. Use a copy of the pattern to copy the hourglass and cut it out.

Card 2

Card: night blue P41 (14.8 x 21 cm), ice blue P42 (14.2 x 10 cm) and white (13 x 8.5 cm) • Pattern 11 • 2 cm wide strips from 4 sheets of Iris folding paper (aqua, blue and de luxe pastels sets) • Silver holographic paper • Fountain corner punch

After punching the card, stick pieces of holographic paper behind the fountains.

Card 3

Card: red (14.8 x 21 cm), mustard yellow P48 (13.9 x 9.3 cm) and cream P27 (13 x 8.5 cm) • Pattern 11 • 2 cm wide strips from 3 envelopes (grey, bronze and burgundy) and from 1 sheet of Iris folding paper (de luxe pastels set) • Gold holographic paper • Borders and Corners Red Oak paper

1.

2.

3.

4.

5.

6.

Card 4

*Card: white (14.8 x 21 cm and 13.5 x 9.1 cm),
Christmas red P43 (14.2 x 9.9 cm) and metallic
aubergine P146 (14 x 9.7 cm) • Pattern 12 • 5 groups
of 2 cm wide strips from 2 red envelopes, from 1
sheet of Iris folding paper (de luxe flowers) and
from 1 red Iris folding greetings sheet • Red paper
(5 x 5 cm) for the stem • Silver holographic paper
• Leaf mini punch*
Cut the glass out of the white card. After finishing
the Iris folding, stick the stem and the leaves on
the front of the card.

Card 5

*Card: orange P11 (14.8 x 21 cm), Perla golden
yellow P141 (14.3 x 10 cm) and lemon C101 (13.8 x
9.5 cm) • Pattern 12 • 5 groups of 2 cm wide strips
from 1 yellow envelope and from 3 sheets of Iris
folding paper (yellow, orange and de luxe flowers
sets) • Yellow paper (5 x 5 cm) • Gold holographic
paper • Iris folding text -sticker • Fountain corner
punch*

Card 6

*Card: heather P22 (14.8 x 21 cm) and Christmas
red P43 (13.4 x 8.9 cm) • Pattern 12 • 5 groups
of 2 cm wide strips from 1 pink envelope and
from 3 sheets of Iris folding paper (orange, red
and de luxe colourful sets) • Pink paper (5 x 5 cm)
• Silver holographic paper • Star border ornament
punch*

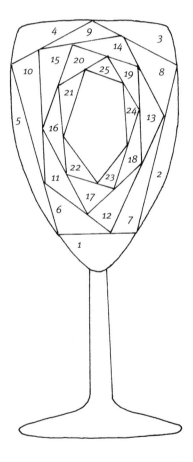

Pattern 12 - Wine glass

Cards based on the diamond

Diamonds

All the cards are made according to the instructions given for the basic pattern (see Techniques).

Card 1 - Basic pattern

Card: white 14.8 x 21 cm and violet 13.5 x 8 cm (P20) • Pattern 1 • 2 cm wide strips: red envelope, dark blue envelope, blue lily origami paper (12103 from O-E) and red castles (13 vrs 007 from D) • Silver holographic paper

Cut the diamond out of the smallest card. After completing the Iris folding, cut a red strip and a blue strip (13.5 x 2 cm). Use photo glue to stick the strips on the card so that 0.4 cm protrudes over the edge and stick it on the double card.

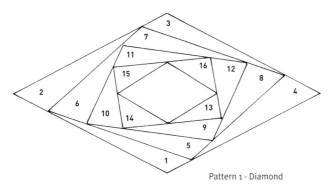

Pattern 1 - Diamond

Card 2

Card: Christmas red 14.8 x 21 cm (P43), night blue 13.5 x 9 cm (P41) and white 13 x 8 cm • Pattern 1 • 2 cm wide strips: 2x dark blue Japanese paper and 2x gold IF paper (green set) • Gold holographic paper

Fill alternate sections with gold and dark blue paper.

Card 3

Card: night blue 14.8 x 21 cm (P41), white 13.4 x 8.5 cm and fiesta red 12.8 x 8 cm (P12) • Pattern 1 • 2 cm wide strips: 2x blue/white Japanese paper and 2x blue envelope • Silver holographic paper • Multi-corner punch

Card 4

Card: white 14.8 x 21 cm and dark blue 13.5 x 9 cm (cA417) • Pattern 1 • 2 cm wide strips: 2x blue IF paper, light blue envelope and blue flower pattern (ts 14 from D) • Silver holographic paper • Multi-corner punch

Punch two corners of the blue card and cut the diamonds out of the back 1 cm from the side and 1.2 cm from the top and bottom.

1.

2.

3.

4.

5.

6.

Card 5

Card: old red 14.8 x 21 cm (cA517), gold 13 x 8.5 cm (P102) and white 13 x 8.5 cm • Pattern 2 • 2 cm wide strips: 2x green IF paper, 2x orange IF paper and 4x Florentijn paper in various colours (22 crt 012 from D) • Gold holographic paper

Cut the diamonds out of the white card 1.2 cm from all the sides. Put a dot 1.5 cm from the top right-hand corner and bottom left-hand corner and cut all the sides of the card at an angle from these points. Fold a strip of Florentijn paper (6 x 1.4 cm) so that it measures 6 x 0.6 cm and use it to cover both no. 1 sections. Continue the Iris folding as explained for the basic model.

Card 6

Card: goldline 14.8 x 21 cm (P301), dark red 13.5 x 8.8 cm (cA519) and white 12 x 8 cm • Pattern 1 • 2 cm wide strips: aqua IF paper, 2x aqua Florentijn paper (12063 from O-E) and gold origami paper (13031 from O-E) • Gold holographic paper • Art Deco corner scissors

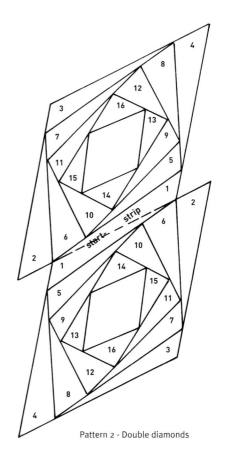

Pattern 2 - Double diamonds

Duck and bib

The duck is made according to the instructions given for card 1 and the bib is made according to the instructions given for card 3.

paper for the head (section 2) double. Cut the water, use the hole punch to punch the eye and stick them on the card.

Card 1

Card: warm pink 14.8 x 21 cm (cA485), white 13.5 x 9 cm and light blue 11 x 8.3 cm (cA391) • Pattern 3 • 2 cm wide strips: pink origami paper (13008 from O-E), petrol IF paper (aqua set) and 2x aqua Florentijn paper (12063 from O-E) • 5 x 4 cm piece of pink paper for the head • Gold holographic paper • Multi-corner punch • Hole punch

Punch the bottom corners of the white and blue card and cut the duck out of the blue card. Fold the

Card 2

Card: violet 14.8 x 21 cm (cA425), soft yellow 13 x 9.3 cm and lavender 12.6 x 9 cm (cA487) • Pattern 3 • 2 cm wide strips: yellow envelope, purple origami paper (12031 from O-E), green duck and green waffle (13 vrs 015 and cp 187 from D) • 5 x 4 cm piece of yellow paper for the head • Gold holographic paper • Multi-corner punch • Hole punch

Card 3

Card: white 14.8 x 21 cm, light blue 13.4 x 9.4 cm (cA391) and pink 13 x 9 cm (cA481) • Pattern 4 • 2 cm wide strips: 3x paper with flowers (7 pai 4545 from D) and 3x light blue envelope • Silver holographic paper • Multi-corner punch • Hole punch

Punch two corners of the pink card and cut out the bib. Use flower strips to fill all the A sections from the top downwards. Use light blue strips to fill all the B sections from the top downwards.

Use light blue strips and flower strips alternately to fill the other sections. Use foam tape to stick the pink card on the light blue card. Stick the press stud in the top left-hand corner of the bib.

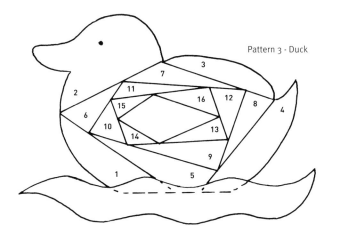

Pattern 3 - Duck

Card 4

*Card: ice blue 14.8 x 21 cm (P42), dark pink 14 x 9.7 cm
(C352) and white 13.5 x 9.4 cm • Pattern 4 • 2 cm
wide strips: 2x blue grey IF paper (aqua set), pink
envelope, red envelope and 2x flower paper • Gold
holographic paper • 3-in-1 corner punch - Heart*
The strips for sections A and 1, 5, 9, etc. are flowered.
The strips for sections B and 2, 6, 10, etc. are blue
grey.

Card 5

*Card: white 14.8 x 21 cm, light blue 12.8 x 9 cm
(C490) and mint 12 x 9 (8.3) cm (cA331) • Pattern 3
• 2 cm wide strips: 4x aqua IF paper • 5 x 4 cm
piece of aqua paper for the head • Silver holographic
paper • Border ornament punch - Rope • Hole
punch*

Card 6

*Card: peach 14.8 x 21 cm, warm pink 12.7 x 9 cm
(cA485) and light pink 12 x 8.4 cm (C103) • Pattern
3 • 2 cm wide strips: 3x pink origami paper (13008,
13039 and 13045 from O-E) and beige envelope
• 5 x 4 cm pink origami paper for the head • Bronze
holographic paper • Multi-corner punch • Hole
punch*

Pattern 4 - Bib

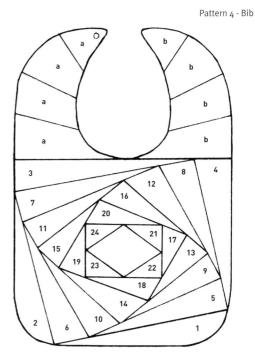

Trees and flowers

The tree is made according to the instructions given for card 1 and the cornflower is made according to the instructions given for card 3.

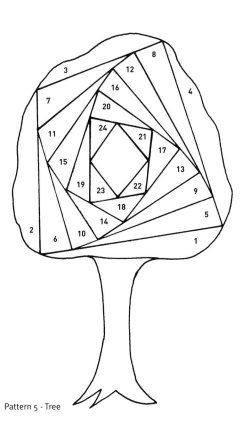

Pattern 5 - Tree

Card 1

Card: cerise 14.8 x 21 cm (P33), Christmas green 14 x 9.5 cm (P18) and white 13.4 x 9 cm • Pattern 5 • 2 cm wide strips: green IF paper, green leaf origami paper (12103 from O-E), green envelope and green/beige Tassotti paper (1715 from V) • 5 x 3 cm piece of green paper for the trunk and 3 x 2 cm piece of red paper for the apples • Green holographic paper • Figure punch - Apple • Corner punch - Apple

Punch the corners of the white card. Cut out the crown of the tree and fill it with strips. Cut the trunk, punch the apples and stick them on the card.

Card 2

Card: violet 14.8 x 21 cm (P20), lime green 13 x 9 cm (P188) and white 12.5 x 8.5 cm • Pattern 5 • 2 cm wide strips: 2x green IF paper, lilac IF paper (purple set) and purple lavender branches (7 tas 1731 from D) • Purple holographic paper • Corner punch - Spear

Card 3

Card: fresh green 13 x 26 cm (P130), fern green 11.5 x 11.5 cm (P137) and white 11 x 11 cm • Pattern 6 • 3 cm wide strips: 4x yellow origami paper (12012, 12023, 13008 and 13037 from O-E) • Gold holographic paper • 3-in-1 corner punch - Flowers

Punch the corners of the white card and cut out the flower. Stick small pieces of double-sided adhesive tape to the back of the card near the four small crosses. Fill the cornflower with strips.

Card 4

Card: mustard yellow 13 x 26 cm (P48), water blue 11 x 11 cm (P131) and soft yellow 10.5 x 10.5 cm (P132) • Pattern 6 • 3 cm wide strips: 4x blue IF paper • Silver holographic paper • 3-in-1 corner punch - Leaves

Card 5

Card: cerise 13 x 26 cm (P33), bright pink 11 x 11 cm, Christmas red 10.6 x 10.6 cm (P43) and blossom 10.2 x 10.2 cm (P34) • Pattern 6 • 3 cm wide strips: 4x pink carnation origami paper (12012, 12027, 1254 and 13039, from O-E) • Red holographic paper

Card 6

Card: mustard yellow 14.8 x 21 cm (P48), dark blue 13 x 9 cm (P06) and white 12.5 x 8.5 cm • Pattern 5 • 2 cm wide strips: yellow IF paper, green origami paper (13045 from O-E) and 2x tulip paper (cp 931 from D) • Gold holographic paper • 3-in-1 corner punch - Flowers

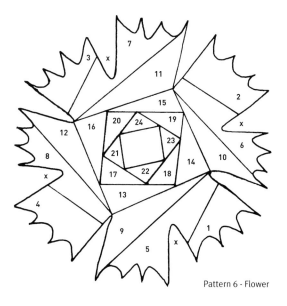

Pattern 6 - Flower

Sweet jar

All the cards are made according to the instructions given for card 1.

Card 1

Card: water blue 14.8 x 21 cm (P131), old red 12.3 x 9.6 cm (cA517) and soft yellow 11.7 x 9.2 cm (P132) • Pattern 7 • 2 cm wide strips: 2x blue IF paper, forget-me-not blue and plaited red (cp 712 and cp 174 from D) and red envelope • Silver holographic paper • 3-in-1 corner punch - Flowers
Punch the top corners of the yellow card. Cut out the jar without the lid or the base and fill the jar with strips. Cut the lid and the base out of blue IF paper and stick them on the card. Decorate the card with a flower. Use foam tape to stick the yellow card on the red card.

Card 2

Card: cherry red 14.8 x 21 cm (P133), white 13 x 9.7 cm and orange 12.5 x 9.2 cm (P135) • Pattern 7 • 2 cm wide strips: 2x green envelopes, yellow checked IF paper (yellow set), cherry paper and apple paper (both fruit paper from V) • Bronze holographic paper • Butterfly corner punch

Card 3

Card: spring green 14.8 x 21 cm (cA305), rust 12.8 x 9.6 cm (C504) and soft yellow 11.7 x 9.2 cm (P132) • Pattern 7 • 2 cm wide strips: green envelope, yellow envelope, brown IF

paper (yellow set) and 2x mini cakes (10 pai 4487 from D) • Gold holographic paper • 3-in-1 corner punch - Lace

Card 4

Card: yellow 14.8 x 21 cm (cA275), dark red 13.2 x 9.7 cm (cA519) and white 12.7 x 9.4 cm • Pattern 7 • 2 cm wide strips: paper with sweets (pink

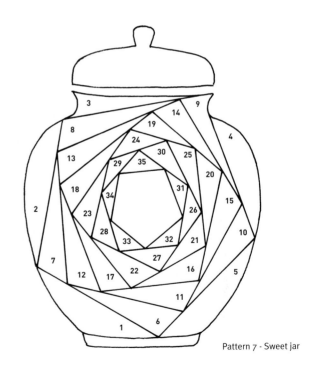

Pattern 7 - Sweet jar

carnation, aqua, orange, green and yellow)
(10 tas 204 from D) and pink carnation envelope
paper • Gold holographic paper • Corner scissors
- Nostalgia
Use the corner scissors to cut two corners of the
white card and cut out the jar. After completing
the Iris folding, stick half a sweet on the card.

Card 5

*Card: apple green 14.8 x 21 cm (C475), lime green
12.5 x 9.4 cm (P188) and white 11.2 x 9 cm • Pattern 7
• 2 cm wide strips: 3x green IF paper, blue IF paper
and blue envelope • Green holographic paper
• 3-in-1 corner punch - Lace*

Card 6

*Card: cream 14.8 x 21 cm (cA241), golden yellow
12.4 x 9.4 cm (cA247) and violet 12 x 9 cm (P20)
• Pattern 7 • 2 cm wide strips: 2x yellow IF paper,
purple IF paper, beige envelope and purple
envelope • Gold holographic paper • Circle template*
Draw five circles (Ø 1.7 cm) for the lollies and cut
1.5 mm wide cream pieces of card for the sticks.

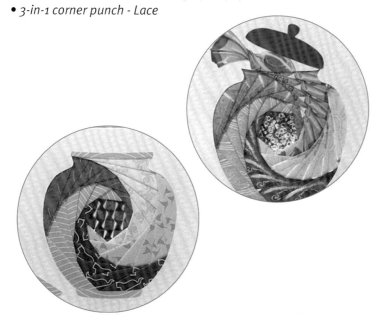

Dragonfly

All the cards are made according to the instructions given for card 1.

Card 1 (card on the cover)

Card: mustard yellow 13 x 26 cm (P48), dark green 12 x 12 cm (cA309) and white 11.5 x 11.5 cm • Pattern 8 • 1.5 cm wide strips: dark green IF paper (petrol set), yellow envelope and Florentijn paper in various colours (22 crt 001 from D) • 8 x 3 cm piece of green paper for the body • Gold holographic paper • 3-in-1 corner punch - Bugs

Punch the top right-hand corner of the white card. Only cut the wings out of the back of the white card and fill them with strips.

Use a light box to copy the body and stick it on the front of the card.

Card 2

Card: cornflower blue 13 x 26 cm (cA393), mauve 12 x 11.5 cm (P13), warm pink 12 x 10.5 cm (cA485) and white 11.5 x 10 cm • Pattern 8 • 1.5 cm wide strips: red envelope, aqua IF paper and aqua Colourful de luxe IF paper • 8 x 3 cm piece of red envelope for the body • Silver holographic paper • 3-in-1 corner punch - Flowers

Card 3

Card: royal blue 13 x 26 cm (P136), azure 12 x 12 cm (P04) and white 11.5 x 11.5 cm • Pattern 8 • 1.5 cm wide strips: 2x blue envelope and sea green envelope • 8 x 3 cm piece of blue paper for the body • Sea green holographic paper • Border ornament punch - Rope

Cut the top right-hand and bottom left-hand corner of the white card at an angle 0.5 cm from the corner and punch a border in the top right-hand corner and the bottom left-hand corner.

Card 4

*Card: golden yellow 13 x 26 cm (cA247), grey green
11.8 x 11.8 cm and white 11.3 x 11.3 cm • Pattern 8
• 1.5 cm wide strips: 2x petrol IF paper and gold IF
paper (yellow set) • 8 x 3 cm piece of petrol paper
for the body • Green holographic paper • Gold decorative line stickers no. 4 • Corner scissors - Celestial*
Cut three corners of the white card and cut out the
wings. Decorate the card with the line stickers.

Tip:
*If you wish to know what the effect of
the different colours will be before you
start, make a copy of the pattern and use
coloured pencils to colour it in. You will
then quickly see what it will look like.*

Pattern 8 - Dragonfly

Cross pattern

All the cards are made according to the instructions given for card 1.

Card 1

Card: ochre 14.8 x 21 cm (cA575) and cream 10.2 x 9.4 cm (cA241) • Parchment: dark yellow 14.8 x 10 cm (1644) • Pattern 9 • 1.5 cm wide strips: dark brown IF paper (orange set), light brown IF paper (yellow set) and old pink/beige Tassotti (1714 from V) • 10 x 2 cm piece of dark brown paper • Gold holographic paper • Border ornament punch - Lace

Cut the four sections out of the smallest card and fill them with strips. Draw one triangle on the piece of brown paper (10 x 2 cm) and fold the strip double twice. Use a staple to keep it in place and cut the four triangles in one go. Stick them on the front of the card. Use the border ornament punch to decorate the top and bottom of the parchment.

Card 2

Card: dark blue 13 x 26 cm (cA417), light blue 11 x 11 cm (C490) and shell white 10.5 x 10.5 cm (C112) • Pattern 9 • 1.5 cm wide strips: blue envelope, grey green origami paper (13039 from O-E) and blue vine (cp 81 from D) • 10 x 2 cm piece of blue paper for the triangles • Silver holographic paper • 3-in-1 corner punch - Lace

Card 3

Card: pale pink 13 x 26 cm and 10.5 x 10.5 cm (cA480), salmon 11.5 x 11.5 cm (cA482) and terracotta 11 x 11 cm (cA549) • Pattern 9 • 1.5 cm wide strips: brown origami paper (11008 from O-E), grey envelope and brown grey cord pattern (mg 010 from D) • 10 x 2 cm piece of brown paper for the triangles • Gold holographic paper • 3-in-1 corner punch - Leaves

Card 4

Card: wine red 14.8 x 21 cm (P36), twilight grey 14 (13) x 9.2 cm (C131) and pale pink 10.5 x 9.2 cm (cA480) • Pattern 9 • 1.5 cm wide strips: 3x purple

IF paper • *10 x 2 cm piece of purple paper for the triangles • Silver holographic paper • Border ornament punch - Leaf*

Cut the four sections out of the smallest card and use the border ornament punch to decorate the top and bottom of the grey card.

Card 5

Card: dark green 14.8 x 21 cm (cA309) and cream 12.5 x 9.5 cm (cA241) • Pattern 9 • 1.5 cm wide strips: green IF paper, denim green origami paper (1254 from O-E) and green/beige Tassotti (1715 from V) • 10 x 2 cm piece of green paper for the triangles • Gold holographic paper • 3-in-1 corner punch - Leaves

Pattern 9 - Cross pattern

Christmas decorations and candles

The Christmas decorations are made according to the instructions given for the card on the cover and the candle is made according to the instructions given for card 4.

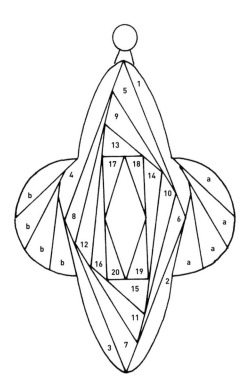

Pattern 10 - Christmas decoration

Card on the cover

Card: ochre 14.8 x 21 cm (cA575), dark green 13 x 9 cm (cA309) and white 12.5 x 8.5 cm • Pattern 10 • 2 cm wide strips: yellow IF paper, green IF paper and green/beige Tassotti (1715 from V) • Gold holographic paper • Corner scissors - Nostalgia

Decorate the corners of the white card with part of the scissors and cut the Christmas decoration out. Cut the eye out of green paper and stick it on the card. Use foam tape to stick the white card on the green card.

Card 1

Card: Iris blue 14.8 x 21 cm (P31) and white 13 x 9 cm • Silver holographic paper - Honey-comb (EmJe) 13.3 x 9.3 cm • Pattern 10 • 2 cm wide strips: 2x sea green gift paper, 2x purple gift paper and 2x honeycomb silver holographic paper • Silver holographic paper • 3-in-1 corner punch - Snowflakes

Card 2

Card: dark green 14.8 x 21 cm (cA309), cerise 13 x 9 cm (P33) and white 12.5 x 8.5 cm • Pattern 10 • 2 cm wide strips: green IF paper (petrol set), green beige Tassotti (1715 from V) and yellow envelope • Pink square holographic paper • 10 cm of pink thread • Corner scissors - Nostalgia

Card 3

Card: violet 14.8 x 21 cm (P20) and white 12.2 x 8.7 cm • Dark red envelope 12.8 x 9.2 cm • Pattern 10 • 2 cm wide strips: 2x purple gift paper, 2x dark red envelope and 2x holly silver holographic paper (EmJe) • Purple holographic paper • 3-in-1 corner punch - Lace

Card 4

Card: red, triple square aperture card 14.8 x 21 cm (192-23 from R) and red 14.5 x 10.2 cm • Pattern 11 • 1 cm wide strips: 2x beige leaf origami paper (14040), gold and red/beige stripes (both 13031

from O-E) • 6 x 3 cm piece of gold paper and
4.5 x 2 cm piece of leaf paper for the flames
• Gold holographic paper • Gold decorative line
stickers no. 4

Fill each square with strips and cover the back
with the single card. Copy the big flame onto
the strip of gold paper. Fold it into three and cut
out the flames in one go. Make the small flames
in the same way. Stick the line stickers and the
flames on the card.

Card 5

*Card: blue, triple square aperture card 14.8 x
21 cm (192-25 from R) and blue 14.5 x 10.2 cm
• Pattern 11 • 1 cm wide strips: 2x lilac gift paper
and 2x blue flower pattern (ts 14 from D) • 6 x
3 cm piece of lilac paper for the flames • Silver
holographic paper*

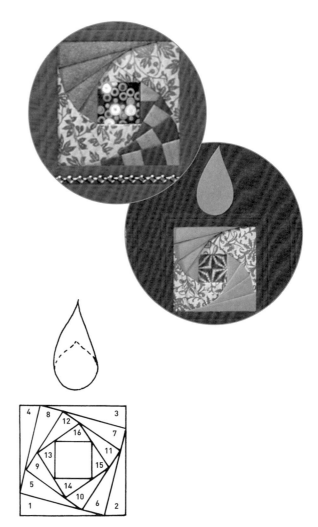

Pattern 11 - Candle

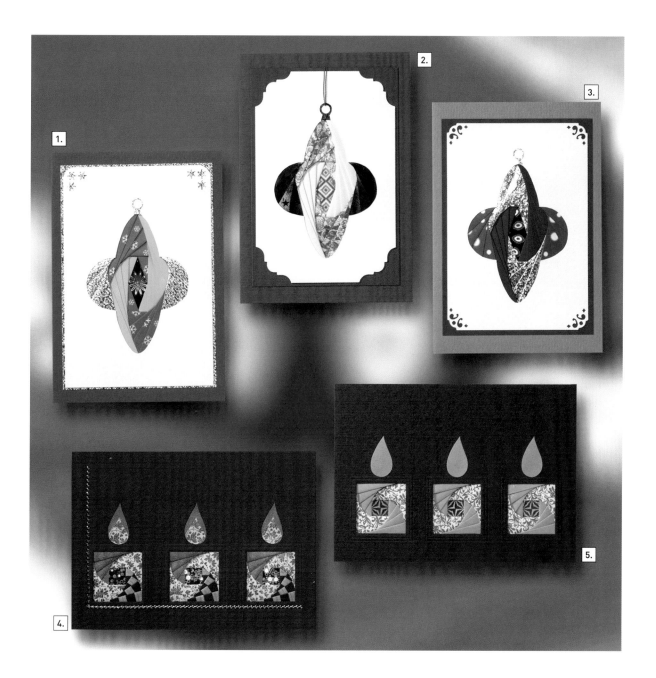

CHRISTMAS DECORATIONS AND CANDLES 63

Small star and robin redbreast

The star is made according to the instructions given for card 1 and the robin redbreast is made according to the instructions given for card 4.

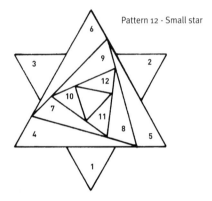

Pattern 12 - Small star

Card 1

Card: blue 13 x 26 cm, mustard yellow 10.5 x 10.5 cm (P48), pale yellow 10 x 10 cm and dark blue 8 x 8 cm (C500) • Pattern 12 • 2 cm wide strips: yellow envelope, pale yellow envelope and gold paper (V)
Cut out the star from the smallest card.

Card 2

Card: dark blue 13 x 26 cm (P06), white 10 x 10 cm, turquoise 7.3 x 7.3 cm (P32) and mustard yellow 7 x 7 cm (P48) • 10 x 10 cm pale yellow parchment (1645) • 2 cm wide strips: white envelope, blue envelope and sea green gift paper
• Silver holographic paper • Border punch - Star
Punch all the borders of the parchment and stick it on the white card.

Card 3

Card: cream 13 x 26 cm (cA241), dark blue 11 x 11 cm (cA417) and violet 7.2 x 7.2 cm (P20) • Pattern 12 • 2 cm wide strips: yellow envelope, beige envelope and yellow IF paper • Gold holographic paper • Gold decorative line stickers no. 4 • 3-in-1 corner punch - Celestial

Card 4

Card: dark red 14.8 x 21 cm (cA519), ochre 12.2 x 8.4 cm (cA575) and white 11 x 8 cm • Pattern 13 • 2 cm wide strips: orange envelope, grey white envelope and brown grey cable pattern (mg 010 from D) • Black paper for the eye and beak • Gold holographic paper • Hole punch • Black fine-liner • Corner punch - Holly

Punch two corners of the white card and cut out the bird without the beak. Use a light box to copy the feet onto the back of the card. Turn the card over and use a fine-liner to draw them on the front of the card. Sections 1A, 1B, 4A, 4B, 4C, 7A, 7B and 10 are brown grey, sections 2, 5, 8, 11A and 11B are orange and sections 3, 6A, 6B, 9A, 9B, 12A, 12B and 12C are grey white. Use the hole punch to punch the eye, cut out a beak and stick them on the card. Use foam tape to stick the white card on the ochre card.

Card 5

Card: ochre 14.8 x 21 cm, dark blue 11.3 x 9.4 cm (P06), orange 10.7 x 8.9 cm (cA545) and white 10.2 x 8.5 cm • Pattern 13 • 2 cm wide strips: grey white envelope, brown origami paper (12054 from O-E) and orange origami paper (12031 from O-E) • Bronze holographic paper • Corner punch - Carl

Card 6

Card: dark chestnut 14.8 x 21 cm (C501), raw sienna 12 x 9 cm (C374), red earth 10 x 9 cm (C130) and white 10 (8.8) x 9 cm • Pattern 13 • 2 cm wide strips: brown IF paper (orange set), grey envelope and orange envelope • Silver holographic paper
• Border ornament punch - Holly

Card on page 41

Card: dark blue 14.8 x 21 cm (C500), rust 11.5 x 9.2 cm, mustard yellow 10.7 x 8.3 cm (P48) and white 10.8 (9.6) x 8.3 cm • Pattern 13 • 2 cm wide strips: grey white envelope, orange origami paper (12031 from O-E) and brown IF paper (orange set) • Mother-of-pearl holographic paper
• Border ornament punch - Holly

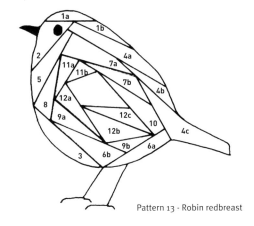

Pattern 13 - Robin redbreast

Cards based on the basic shape

Basic shape

Colourful cards with bright

flower pots.

All the cards are made according to the instructions given for the basic shape (see Techniques).

Card 1

Card: light Havana C502 (14.8 x 21 cm) and white (13.8 x 10 cm) • Pattern 1 • 2 cm wide strips from 2 beige envelopes and 2 sheets of Iris folding paper (yellow set) • 2 pieces of green paper (3 x 10 cm) for the plant • Gold holographic paper • 3-in-1 corner punch (flower)

Punch the corners of the white card and cut out the pot. Fill the pot with strips. Copy the plant onto a piece of green paper (see page 70). Place the second piece of green paper on the other piece of paper and staple them together. Cut the plants out and stick them above the pot.

Card 2

Card: Structura sunflower P134 (14.8 x 21 cm), corn-flower A425 (13.7 x 9.5 cm) and white (13.3 x 9 cm) • Pattern 1 • 4 groups of 2 cm wide strips from 3 yellow envelopes • Piece of grey envelope paper (6 x 9 cm) • 2 cm wide yellow strips of Iris folding paper de luxe (pastels set) • Gold holographic paper

• Figure scissors (heartstrings) • Flowers from a hand punch

Use the figure scissors to cut the strips of Iris folding paper de luxe into 1 cm wide strips. Lay one half aside and add the other half to the group of colour C. Place the yellow strips up to the dotted line and then place the strips cut with the figure scissors on top up to the line of section 3. Also do this for sections 7, 11, 15 and 19.

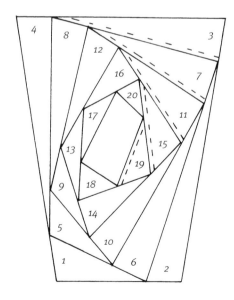

Pattern 1 - Basic shape

Card 3

Card: brick red P35 (14.8 x 21 cm) and white (14.1 x 9.6 cm) • Pattern 1 • 2 cm wide strips from four sheets of Iris folding paper (green, orange and yellow sets) • Green paper for the plant (3 x 10 cm) • Gold holographic paper • Corner punch (spear) • Figure punch (flower) • Punch (small flower)

Card 4

Card: ivory C111 (14.8 x 21 cm) and brick red P35 (13.7 x 9.4 cm) • Pattern 1 • 2 cm wide strips from 4 sheets of Iris folding paper (orange and yellow sets) • Silver holographic paper • Photo corner figure punch (flower) • Punch (flower)
After completing the Iris folding, punch the corners of the ivory card and slide the red card behind the flowers.

Card 5

Card: cornflower A425 (14.8 x 21 cm) and Structura fresh green P130 (13.6 x 9.5 cm) • Pattern 1 • 2 cm wide strips from 4 lilac envelopes • 2 cm wide strips of Iris folding paper de luxe (bright set) • Green paper for the branches • Silver holographic paper • 3-in-1 corner punch (leaves) • Figure punch (waves) • Figure punch (branch)

Card 6

Card: cerise P33 (14.8 x 21 cm), Antica green P169 (14.3 x 10 cm) and white (13.8 x 9.5 cm) • Pattern 1 • 2 cm wide strips from 4 sheets of Iris folding paper (red, orange and petrol sets) • Petrol paper (3 x 6 cm) for the cactus • Silver holographic paper • Corner scissors (regal) • Punch (strawberry)

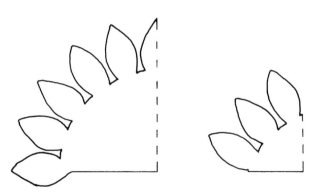

Plant pattern (the basic shape)

1.

2.

3.

4.

5.

6.

Playing with shapes

The jug is full,

so fill the glasses.

The glasses are made according to the instructions given for card 1 and the jug is made according to the instructions given for card 2.

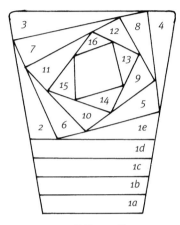

Pattern 2 - Glass

Card 1

Card: lilac A453 (14.8 x 21 cm), pastel green A331 (14.5 x 10 cm and 0.35 x 5 cm for the straws) and white (13.8 x 9.8 cm) • Pattern 2 • 2 cm wide strips from 2 sheets of Iris folding paper (purple and aqua sets) • Silver holographic paper • Fruit from a fruits-of-the-forest teabag • Corner punch (flower)
Punch two corners of the white card. Cut out the glasses and fill them with the strips.
Make a 0.7 cm long incision at the top of each glass for the straws and stick them in place.

Card 2

Card: lobster red A545 (13 x 26 cm), sienna C374 (11.5 x 11.5 cm) and white (10.5 x 10.5 cm) • Pattern 3 • 2 cm wide strips from 3 sheets of Iris folding paper (orange set) and 1 sheet of Iris folding paper de luxe (bright set) • Piece of Iris folding paper de luxe (bright set) (11 x 11 cm) • Gold holographic paper • Die-cut stickers (K&Company)
Cut the jug, but not the handle, out of the white card. Cut the handle out of orange paper.

Card 3

Card: Structura sunflower P134 (14.8 x 21 cm), orange (14 x 9.9 cm) and Structura pale yellow P132 (14 x 9.3 cm) • Pattern 2 • 2 cm wide strips from 1 orange envelope, 2 sheets of Iris folding paper (yellow set) and 1 sheet of Iris folding paper de luxe (pastels set) • Gold holographic paper • 3-in-1 corner punch (celestial) • Lemon from a lemon-flavour teabag • Paper (4.5 x 0.4 cm) for the straw • Bubbles from the art punch

Card 4

Card: pink A481 (14.8 x 21 cm), violet C507 (14 x 10 cm) and white C335 (13 x 9.5 cm) • Pattern 2 • 2 cm wide strips from 4 sheets of Iris folding paper (red and purple sets) • 2 pieces of Iris folding paper de luxe (pastels set) for the straws (0.35 x 5 cm) and the lemon (Ø 2 cm) • Gold holographic paper • 3-in-1 corner punch (celestial)

Card 5

Card: ivory C111 (14.8 x 21 cm and 10.5 x 10.5 cm) and bright yellow C400 (13.9 x 10.5 cm) • Pattern 3 • 2 cm wide strips from 1 yellow envelope, 2 sheets of Iris folding paper (yellow set) and 1 sheet of de luxe Iris folding paper (pastels set) • Gold holographic paper • Figure punch (flower)

Card 6

Card: cerise P33 (14.8 x 21 cm), warm yellow C553 (13.9 x 9.8 cm) and white C110 (13.5 x 9.4 cm) • Pattern 2 • 2 cm wide strips from 3 orange/red/ pink envelopes and 1 sheet of Iris folding paper de luxe (bright set) • Rainbow holographic paper • 3-in-1 corner punch (flowers) • Orange from a orange-flavour teabag • Half a straw

Card 7

Card: fiesta red P12 (13 x 26 cm) and white (11.5 x 11.5 cm) • Pattern 3 • 2 cm wide strips from 1 orange envelope and 3 sheets of Iris folding paper (orange set) • K&Company Romanza ivory embossed paper (12.2 x 12.2 cm) • Silver holographic paper • Border punch (spring)

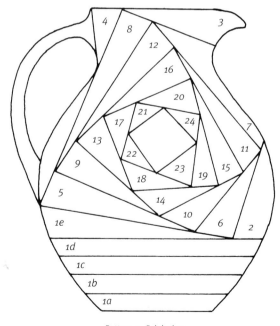

Pattern 3 - Drinks jug

Parasol

Let the sun shine!

All the parasols are made according to the instructions given for card 1.

Card 1

Card: royal blue A427 (14.8 x 21 cm) and Structura orange P135 (14.8 x 10 cm) • Pattern 4 • 4 groups of 2 cm wide strips from 3 blue envelopes • Silver holographic paper • Figure scissors (heartstrings) • Figure punch (shell)

Use the figure scissors to cut along two edges of the small card. Cut out the parasol without the pole. To make the twinshell, place a folded piece of paper in the punch so that the fold almost touches the top of the shell. Cut the pole out of paper and stick it on the card together with the shells.

Card 2

Card: IRIS blue P31 (13 x 26 cm), green (12.2 x 12.2 cm) and white (11.5 x 11.5 cm) • Pattern 4 • 2 cm wide strips from blue/green envelopes • Silver holographic paper • Embossing stencil (corners) • Iris folding text sticker

Card 3

Card: sunny yellow A247 (14.8 x 21 cm), lemon C101 (13.6 x 10.2 cm) and cornflower blue A425 (13 x 10 cm) • Pattern 4 • 2 cm wide strips from

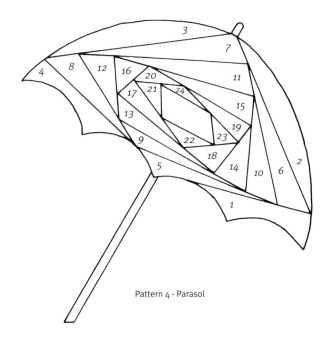

Pattern 4 - Parasol

2 orange envelopes and 2 sheets of Iris folding paper (yellow and orange sets) • Gold holographic paper • 3-in-1 corner punch (celestial)

Card 4

Card: fiesta red P12 (13 x 26 cm), sunny yellow A247 (12 x 12 cm) and Structura pale yellow P132 (11.6 x 11.6 cm) • Pattern 4 • 2 cm wide strips from one envelope and 3 sheets of Iris folding paper (red, orange and yellow sets) • Gold holographic paper • Iris folding text sticker • Border ornament punch (wave)

Card 5

Card: lobster red A545 (13 x 26 cm), Structura fern green P137 (12 x 12 cm) and white (11.8 x 11.8 cm) • Pattern 4 • 2 cm wide strips from 4 sheets of Iris folding paper (yellow and orange sets) • Silver holographic paper • Embossing stencil (garden) • Background embossing stencil AE 1201 • Punch (shell)

Card 7

Card: yellow A275 (14.8 x 21 cm) and violet P20 (13.5 x 10 cm) • Pattern 4 • 2 cm wide strips from 2 envelopes and 2 sheets of Iris folding paper (yellow set) • Gold holographic paper • Iris folding text sticker • Border ornament punch (rope)

Card 6

Card: Iris blue P31 (13 x 26 cm), apple green C475 (11.6 x 11.6 cm) and Structura fresh green P130 (11 x 11 cm) • Pattern 4 • 2 cm wide strips from 2 reddish brown and blue envelopes, 1 sheet of Iris folding paper (yellow set) and 1 purple Iris folding greetings sheet • Gold holographic paper

Cats and dogs

Cuddly, trustworthy friends

for young and old.

The cat is made according to the instructions given for card 1 and the dog is made according to the instructions given for card 2. Use a light box to copy the eyes, mouth and nose with a black fine-liner.

Card 1 (on the cover)
Card: salmon C384 (13 x 26 cm), Structura orange P135 (12 x 12 cm) and white C335 (11 x 11 cm) • Pattern 5 • 2 cm wide strips from 4 sheets of Iris folding paper (orange and yellow sets) • Colour B (3 x 4 cm) for the head • Gold holographic paper • 3-in-1 corner punch (bugs)
Punch the top corners of the white card and cut out the body without the head and the tail. Fill the body with the strips of paper. Stick the other parts to the body.

Card 2
Card: white C335 (13 x 26 cm and 13 x 11.8 cm), dark chestnut C501 (12. 7 x 12.7 cm) and Havana brown C502 (12.3 x 12.3 cm) • Pattern 6 • 2 cm wide strips from 3 brown envelopes and 1 sheet of Iris folding paper (yellow set) • Brown paper (3 x 4 cm) for the head • Gold holographic paper • Border punch (rope)

Punch the edges of the small white card and cut out the body without the head and the tail. Note: colour A stops after section 17!

Card 3
Card: bright red C506 (13 x 26 cm and 11.8 x 11.8 cm), gold P102 (12.5 x 12.5 cm) and white C335 (11.5 x 11.5 cm) • Pattern 5 • 2 cm wide strips from 4 grey envelopes • Grey paper (3 x 4 cm) for the head • Gold holographic paper • 3-in-1 corner punch (hearts)

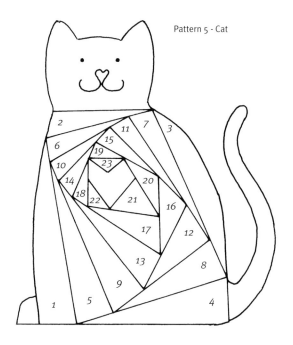

Pattern 5 - Cat

Card 4

Card: sandy yellow C407 (13 x 26 cm) and cerise P33 (11.5 x 11.5 cm) • Pattern 6 • 4 groups of 2 cm wide strips from 3 beige/yellow envelopes • Pale green envelope paper (12 x 12 cm) • Yellow paper (3 x 4 cm) for the head • Gold holographic paper • Puppies from a hand punch • Bones from a border punch

Card 5

Card: white (13 x 26 cm), rust C504 (12.7 x 12.7 cm) and salmon C384 (12.4 x 12.4 cm) • Pattern 5 • 2 cm wide strips from 4 reddish orange envelopes • Red envelope paper (3 x 4 cm) for the head • Bronze holographic paper • 2-in-1 border punch (paw)

Card 6

Card: brick red P35 (13 x 26 cm), metallic bronze (12.1 x 12.1 cm) and white C335 (11.5 x 11.5 cm) • Pattern 6 • 2 cm wide strips from 2 brown envelopes and 2 sheets of IRIS folding paper (yellow and orange sets) • Gold holographic paper • Iris folding text sticker

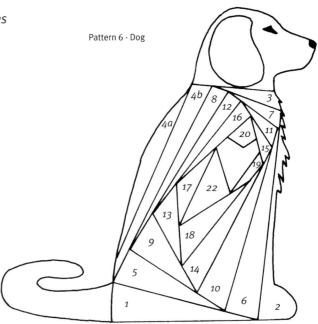

Pattern 6 - Dog

Windmill

A fresh wind turns

the sails.

All the cards are made according to the instructions given for card 1.

Card 1

Card: brick red P35 (13 x 26 cm) and white C111 (12.4 x 12.2 cm) • Pattern 7 • 2 cm wide strips from 1 yellow envelope, 2 sheets of IRIS folding paper (yellow and orange sets) and 1 sheet of Iris folding paper de luxe (flowers set) • Bronze holographic paper • Border ornament punch (heart) • Small hearts from a corner punch (hearts)

Punch the top corners of the white card and cut out the main part of the windmill.
Fill the windmill with strips as described for the basic shape. Copy the top of the windmill and stick it 0.4 cm above the windmill. Staple together four strips of yellow envelope paper (2 x 8 cm) and a copy of one windmill sail. Cut the four sails out at the same time and stick them on the card.
Decorate the card with hearts from the punch.

Card 2

Card: bright yellow C400 (13 x 26 cm) and white (12.4 x 12.1 cm) • Pattern 7 • 2 cm wide strips from 3 green envelopes and 1 sheet of Iris folding paper de luxe (flowers set) • Silver holographic paper • Corner punch (tulip)

Card 3

Card: Structura royal blue P136 (13 x 26 cm) and white (12.5 x 12.5 cm) • Pattern 7 • 2 cm wide strips from 5 blue envelopes • Silver holographic paper • Corner punch (tulip) • Birds from an envelope

Card 4

*Card: burgundy (13 x 26 cm), bright red C506
(12.5 x 12.3 cm), white C335 (12.5 x 11.8 cm) and
4 pieces of cerise paper P33 (2 x 8 cm) for the
sails • Pattern 7 • 2 cm wide strips from 4 red
envelopes • Silver holographic paper • Figure*

*punch (girl) • Balloons from a 2-in-1 border punch
• 3-in-1 corner punch (hearts)*
To make two girls hand-in-hand, slide a folded piece
of paper sideways into the punch until the fold is
half way across the second hand.

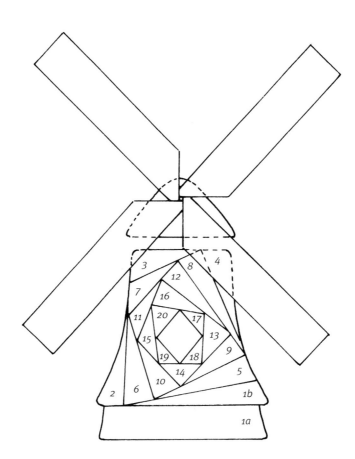

Pattern 7 - Windmill

Baseball cap

Such a hat suits everybody.

All the cards are made according to the instructions given for card 1.

the peak. Fill the cap with strips. Use a light box to copy the peak and the button. Cut them out and stick them on the card. Stick the card on blue paper, then on red paper and finally on the double card.

Card 1

Card: dark blue A417 (14.8 x 21 cm) and white (13.8 x 9 cm) • Pattern 8 • 2 cm wide strips from 2 blue envelopes and 2 sheets of Iris folding paper (blue set) • Blue paper (3 x 6 cm) for the peak • Blue Iris folding paper (14.3 x 9.7 cm) • Red paper (14.6 x 9.7 cm) • Art punch (spear)
Punch the corners of the white card with part of the corner punch and cut out the baseball cap without

Card 2

Card: Structura orange P135 (14.8 x 21 cm) and Irisblue P31 (14.2 x 9.9 cm) • Pattern 8 • 2 cm wide strips from 4 orange, grey, blue and greyish blue envelopes • Orange paper (3 x 6 cm) for the peak • Silver holographic paper • 3-in-1 corner punch (flowers)

Card 3

Card: bright yellow P10 (14.8 x 21 cm) and white (14.3 x 10 cm) • Pattern 8 • 2 cm wide strips from 4 sheets of Iris folding paper (green and yellow sets) • Yellow paper (3 x 6 cm) for the peak • Gold holographic paper • Border ornament punch (rope) • Punch (car) • IRIS folding text sticker

Card 4

Card: grass green P07 (14.8 x 21 cm), Christmas green P18 (14.1 x 9.8 cm) and white C335 (13.7 x 9.4 cm) • Pattern 8 • 2 cm wide strips from 4 green envelopes • Green paper (3 x 6 cm) for the peak • Silver holographic paper • Multi-corner punch

Card 5

Card: dark blue A417 (14.8 x 21 cm), mango A575 (14.5 x 10 cm) and white C335 (14.2 x 9.7 cm) • Pattern 8 • 2 cm wide strips from 4 yellow, orange and blue envelopes • Blue paper (3 x 6 cm) for the peak • Silver holographic paper • Embossing stencil (corners) • Dragonflies from a punch

Card 6

Card: petrol (14.8 x 21 cm) and lavender blue C150 (13.4 x 9 cm) • Pattern 8 • 2 cm wide strips from

4 envelopes (white with text, blue, aqua and green/ blue fishbone) • White envelope paper with text (13.7 x 9.5 cm) • Grey paper (3 x 6 cm) for the peak • Silver holographic paper

Card 7

Card: white C335 (14.8 x 21 cm and 13.6 x 9.3 cm) • Pattern 8 • 2 cm wide strips from 2 grey envelopes and 2 reddish orange envelopes • Envelope paper with text for the peak (5 x 4 cm) • Grey envelope (13.9 x 9.6 cm) plus 2 red edges • Silver holographic paper

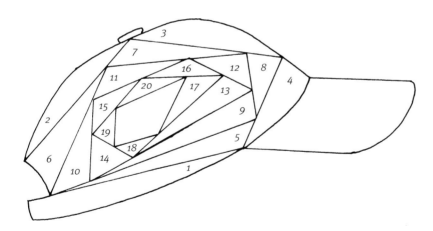

Pattern 8 - Baseball cap

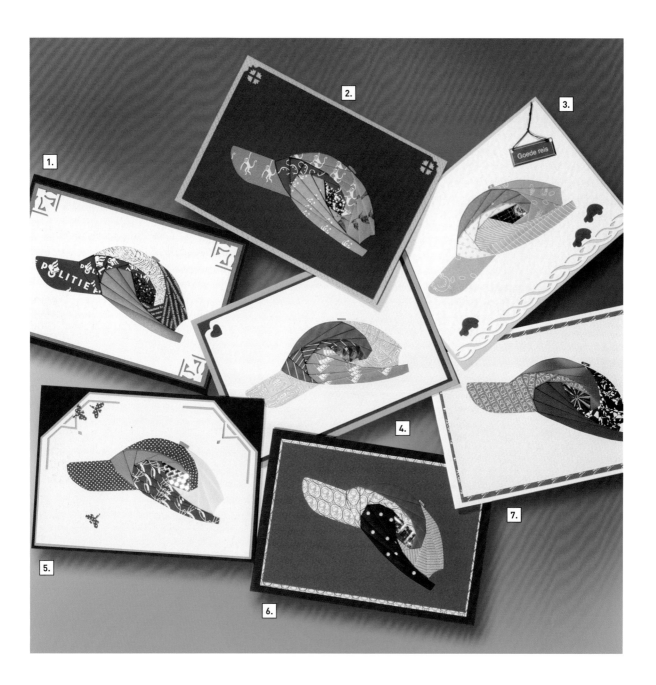

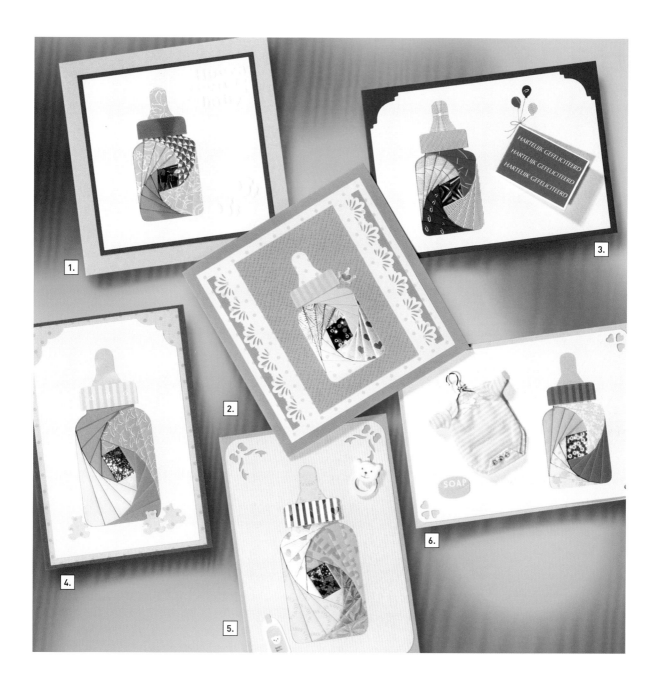

Baby feeding bottles

These baby feeding bottles
will soon be hanging on a line
in the nursery.

The bottles are made according to the instructions given for card 1 and the large patterns are made according to the instructions given for card 4.

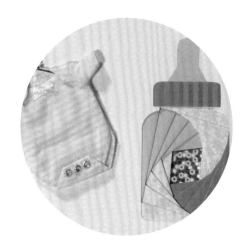

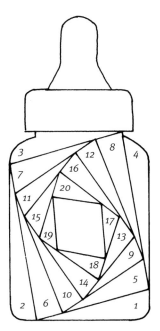

Pattern 9 - Small feeding bottle

Card 1

Card: pink A481 (13 x 26 cm), red A517 (11 x 11 cm) and white (10.4 x 10.4 cm) • Pattern 9 • 4 groups of 2 cm wide strips from 3 different envelopes • Silver holographic paper • Embossing stencil (baby)
Cut the bottle out of white card without the cap or the teat and emboss the shapes on it. Use a light box to copy the cap and the teat. Cut them out and stick them on the card.

Card 2

Card: mango A575 (13 x 26 cm) and Structura orange P135 (10.5 x 7 cm) • Pattern 9 • 2 cm wide strips from 1 sheet of K&Company Peach Dots paper, 1 sheet of Iris folding paper (orange set) and 2 sheets of Iris folding paper de luxe (flowers and pastels sets) • K&Company Peach

Dots paper (11.7 x 11.7 cm) • *Gold holographic paper* • *Border ornament punch (sunburst)* • *Punch (crown)*
Place a 1.1 cm wide pink strip of paper in a Ridge Master and then cut it into the shape of the cap.

Card 3

Card: royal blue A427 (14.8 x 21 cm) and white (14 x 9.7 cm and 3.5 x 10 cm) • *Pattern 9* • *2 cm wide strips from 4 blue envelopes* • *Blue Iris folding greetings sheet (3.2 x 5 cm)* • *Silver holographic paper* • *Balloons from a 2-in-1 border punch* • *Pencil*
Fold the small card double so that it measures 3.5 x 5 cm and stick the greetings sheet on it. Use a pencil to draw strings to tie the balloons to.

Card 4

Card: lavender blue C150 (14.8 x 21 cm) and lemon C101 (13.7 x 8.9 cm) • *Pattern 10* • *2 cm wide strips from 4 blue envelopes* • *Blue envelope (2 x 2.5 cm) for the teat* • *K&Company Romanza citrus paper (14.3 x 9.7 cm)* • *Silver holographic paper* • *Corner scissors (celestial)* • *Figure punch (bear)*

Card 5

Card: apricot P24 (14.8 x 21 cm) and pale pink (14.3 x 10 cm) • *Pattern 10* • *2 cm wide strips from 2 sheets of Iris folding paper (orange set) and 2 sheets of Iris folding paper de luxe (flowers and bright sets)* • *Bronze holographic paper* • *Corner punch (bow)* • *Baby girl outfit from Crea Motion*

Card 6

Card: pink A481 (14.8 x 21 cm) and white (14.3 x 10 cm) • *Pattern 9* • *2 cm wide strips from 2 pink envelopes and 2 sheets of IRIS folding paper (red and purple sets)* • *Silver holographic paper* • *3-in-1 corner punch (hearts)* • *Ridge Master* • *Baby girl outfit from Crea Motion*

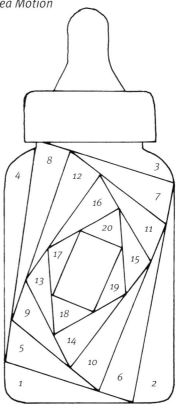

Pattern 10 - Large feeding bottle

4-leaf clovers and strawberries

Lucky four-leaf clovers and

summer fruit.

The four-leaf clover is made according to the instructions given for card 1 and the strawberry is made according to the instructions given for card 2.

Card 1 (card on the cover)

Card: Structura fresh green P130 (14.8 x 21 cm), Christmas green P18 (13 x 9,5 cm) and white C335 (12.5 x 9 cm) • Pattern 11 • 1 cm wide strips from 3 sheets of Iris folding paper (green set) and 1 sheet of Iris folding paper de luxe (pastels set) • Silver holographic paper • Asian sign punch
Turn the punch upside down and punch part of the pattern in the corners of the white card. Cut out the four leaves and fill them with strips. Cut the stem out of green paper and stick it on the card. Cut two strips (9.5 x 1 cm) from pastel green paper and stick them above and below the second card.

Card 2

Card: lily white C110 (13 x 26 cm and 6.5 x 6.5 cm), wine red C503 (9.6 x 9.6 cm) and brick red C505 (8.9 x 8.9 cm) • Pattern 12 • 1.5 cm wide strips from 3 sheets of Iris folding paper (red set) and 1 sheet of Iris folding paper de luxe (bright set) • Green paper (2.5 x 5 cm) • Silver holographic paper
Cut the strawberry, but not the top, out of the white card. Fill the strawberry with strips (see Techniques).

Card 3

Card: pale pink C350 (14.8 x 21 cm), rust brown C504 (13.1 x 9.7 cm) and ivory C111 (12.4 x 10.5 cm) • Pattern 11 • 1 cm wide strips from 3 sheets of Iris folding paper (green and yellow sets) • Gold holographic paper • Border ornament punch (leaves)

Card 4

Card: Structura pale yellow P132 (14.8 x 21 cm), metallic brown P144 (12.8 x 8.5 cm) and lemon C101 (8 x 7 cm) • Pattern 11 • 1 cm wide strips of Iris folding paper (green set) • Gold holographic paper • Rounder corner scissors • Art punch (flower)
Cut the four-leaf clover out of the smallest card and round off the corners. Punch the corners of the brown card.

Card 5

Card: white (14.8 x 21 cm and 14.8 x 6.5 cm) and cerise P33 (14.8 x 7.5 cm) • Pattern 12 • 1.5 cm wide strips from 4 pink/red envelopes • Green paper (2.5 x 5 cm) • Gold holographic paper • Ornare pricking template (Fruit PK 035) • Iris folding text stickers • Punch (strawberry)

Card 6

Card: red A517 (14.8 x 21 cm) and white (14.3 x 10 cm) • Pattern 12 • 1.5 cm wide strips from 2 red envelopes and 2 sheets of Iris folding paper de luxe (Christmas and bright sets) • Green paper (2.5 x 5 cm) • Wekon ladybird vellum (14.8 x 21 cm) • Red holographic paper

Cut the frame out of the vellum (9.5 x 7 cm).

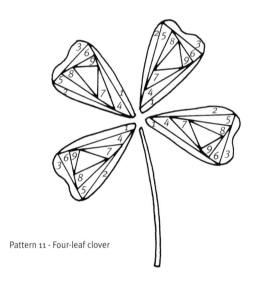

Pattern 11 - Four-leaf clover

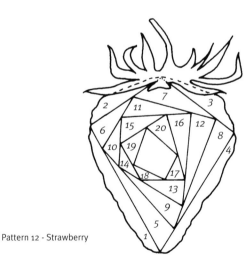

Pattern 12 - Strawberry

Many thanks to:
- *Kars & Co BV in Ochten, the Netherlands*
- *Koninklijke Talens in Apeldoorn, the Netherlands for supplying the card*
- *Em-Je B.V. in Zuidwolde, the Netherlands*
- *Pergamano International in Uithoorn, the Netherlands*
- *Damen, Papier Royaal in The Hague, the Netherlands*
- *Ori-Expres in Reusel, the Netherlands*

The materials used can be ordered by shopkeepers from:
- Avec B.V. in Waalwijk, the Netherlands
- Kars & Co BV in Ochten, the Netherlands
- Papicolor International in Utrecht, the Netherlands.
- Em-Je B.V. in Zuidwolde, the Netherlands
- Pergamano International in Uithoorn, the Netherlands

Card-makers can purchase the paper from:
- Damen, Papier Royaal at Noordeinde 186 in The Hague, the Netherlands (www.papier-royaal.nl)
- Ori-Expres in Reusel, the Netherlands (www.ori-expres.nl)
- Vlieger at Amstel 34 in Amsterdam, the Netherlands

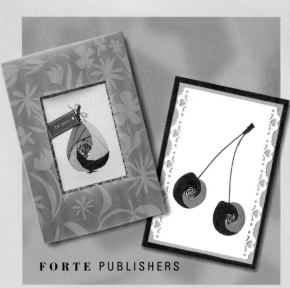

IRIS
Folding
COMPENDIUM

INCLUDING
3 NEW PATTERNS

FORTE PUBLISHERS

Maruscha Gaasenbeek and Tine Beauveser

IRIS
Folding
COMPENDIUM
PART 2

Maruscha Gaasenbeek and Tine Beauveser

FORTE PUBLISHERS

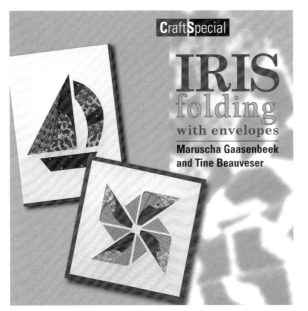

CraftSpecial

IRIS
folding
with envelopes

Maruscha Gaasenbeek
and Tine Beauveser

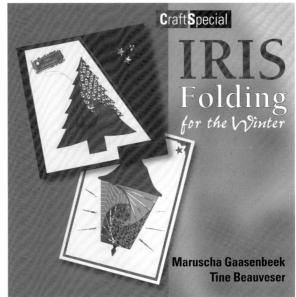

CraftSpecial

IRIS
Folding
for the Winter

Maruscha Gaasenbeek
Tine Beauveser

CraftSpecial

IRIS
folding
with Greetings

Maruscha Gaasenbeek
Tine Beauveser

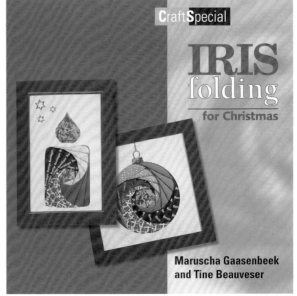

CraftSpecial

IRIS
folding
for Christmas

Maruscha Gaasenbeek
and Tine Beauveser